D0869531

Written
Lives

Also by Javier Marías, Available from New Directions

A HEART SO WHITE

ALL SOULS

DARK BACK OF TIME

THE MAN OF FEELING

TOMORROW IN THE BATTLE THINK ON ME

WHEN I WAS MORTAL

YOUR FACE TOMORROW, VOLUME ONE, FEVER AND SPEAR

Forthcoming:

YOUR FACE TOMORROW, VOLUME TWO, DANCE AND DREAM

YOUR FACE TOMORROW, VOLUME THREE

Written
Lives

Javier Marías

Translated from the Spanish by
MARGARET JULL COSTA

A NEW DIRECTIONS BOOK

Copyright © 1999 by Javier Marías
English translation copyright ©2006 by Margaret Jull Costa

First published in Spain in 2000 as *Vidas Escritas* by Alfaguara, Grupo Santillana de Ediciones,S.A.

Published by arrangement with Mercedes Casanovas Agencia Literaria, Barcelona, and in association with Canongate Books, Ltd., Edinburgh.

The publication of this work has been assisted with a translation subvention from the Director of Books, Archives, and Libraries of the Cultural Ministry of Spain.

The translator would like to thank Javier Marías, Annella McDermott, Antonio Martín, and Ben Sherriff for all their help and advice.

All rights reserved. Except for brief passages quoted in a newspaper, magazine, radio, or television review, no part of this book may be reproduced in any form or by any means, electronic or mechanical, including photocopying and recording, or by any information storage and retrieval system, without permission in writing from the Publisher.

Manufactured in the United States of America
New Directions Books are printed on acid-free paper.
First published clothbound in 2006
Published simultaneously in Canada by Penguin Books Canada Limited
Design by Semadar Megged

Library of Congress Cataloging-in-Publication Data

Marías, Javier.
  [Vidas escritas. English]
  Written lives / Javier Marias ; translated from the Spanish by Margaret Jull Costa.
    p. cm.
  Includes bibliographical references.
  ISBN 0-8112-1611-X (alk. paper)
  1. Authors--Biography. I. Costa, Margaret Jull. II. Title.
  PN466.M3713 2006
  809--dc22

                                        2005015033

New Directions Books are published for James Laughlin
by New Directions Publishing Corporation
80 Eighth Avenue, New York 10011

Contents

Written

Lives

PROLOGUE

THE IDEA FOR THIS book arose from another in which I was also involved: an anthology of very strange stories entitled *Cuentos únicos* (*Unique Tales*—published in 1989 by Ediciones Siruela, Madrid), in which each story was prefaced by a brief biographical note about its extremely obscure author. The majority were so obscure that any information I had about them was sometimes both minimal and difficult to unearth and, therefore, so fragmentary and often so bizarre that it looked as if I had simply invented it all, a conclusion reached by several readers, who, logically enough, also doubted the authenticity of the stories. The fact is that, when read together, these briefest of brief biographies constituted another story, doubtless as unique and spectral as the stories themselves.

I believe, and believed at the time, that this was due not only to the strange and disparate nature of the information available about these ill-fated and forgotten authors, but also to the manner in which the biographies were written, and it occurred to me that I could adopt the same approach with more familiar and more famous writers, about whom, conversely—as befits the age of exhaustive and frequently futile erudition in which we have been living for almost a century now—the curious reader can find out absolutely everything, down to the last detail. The idea, then, was to treat these well-known literary figures as if they were fictional characters, which may well be how all writers, whether famous or obscure, would secretly like to be treated.

The choice of the twenty who appear here was entirely arbitrary (three American, three Irish, two Scottish, two Russian, two French, one Polish, one Danish, one Italian, one German, one Czech, one Japanese, an Englishman from India, and an Englishman from England, if we are going by place of birth). My one condition was that they should all be dead, and I decided, too, to exclude any Spanish writers: on the one hand, I did not want to encroach, however tangentially, on territory that is food and drink to so many of my expert compatriots; on the other hand, some critics and certain fellow indigenous writers have denied my Spanishness on so many and various occasions now (both as regards language and literature and, very nearly, citizenship) that I have, I realise, ended up feeling rather inhibited about discussing writers from my own country—even though these include some of my favourites (March, Bernal Díaz, Cervantes, Quevedo, Torres Villarroel, Larra, Valle-Inclán, Aleixandre, as well as other living authors)—and among whom I continue, despite all, to count myself. But it's as if those critics had convinced me that I had no right to do so, and one acts according to one's convictions.

This book, then, recounts writers' lives or, more precisely, snippets of their lives: I rarely make any judgement about the work, and the sympathy or antipathy with which the characters are treated does not necessarily correspond to any admiration or scorn I might actually feel for their writing. Far from being a hagiography, and far, too, from the solemnity with which artists are frequently treated, these *Written Lives* are told, I think, with a mixture of affection and humour. The latter is doubtless present in every case; the former, I must admit, is lacking in the case of Joyce, Mann, and Mishima.

There is little point in trying to draw conclusions or lay down rules about the lives of writers on the basis of these portraits: what I reveal in them is very partial, and it is precisely in what is included and what omitted that the possible accuracy or inaccuracy of these pieces partly lies. And although almost nothing in them is invented (that is, fictitious in origin), some episodes and anecdotes have been "embellished." Anyway, the one thing that leaps out when you read about these authors is that they were all fairly disastrous individuals; and although they were probably no more so than anyone else whose life we know about, their example is hardly likely to lure one along the path of letters. Luckily, at least—and this should be emphasised—it is clear that none of them took themselves very seriously, apart perhaps from the above-mentioned exceptions, the ones who failed to win my affection. However, I wonder if the lack of seriousness in these texts emanates from the characters themselves or from the views of their accidental, extempore and partial biographer.

For the benefit of the suspicious reader who wants to check some fact or to detect any "embellishments," I provide, at the end, a bibliography, although the said reader will find most of the titles listed very difficult to locate.

This series of *Written Lives* was first published in the magazine *Claves de razón práctica* (nos. 2-21), while the section entitled "Perfect artists," which closes the volume by way of a negative (it is solely about faces and gestures), appeared in the magazine *El Paseante* (no. 17). I am grateful to the editors of the former, Javier Pradera and Fernando Savater, for the gentle and encouraging tyranny they wielded over me and to which the writing of these lives is, in large measure, due.

J.M.
February 1992

This new edition of *Written Lives* contains only a few changes relative to the previous edition, but there is no harm in pointing these out.

A couple of "lives" have been slightly retouched and expanded, the rest remain unchanged. Most of the photographs that precede each "life" are different from those in the 1992 edition (the latter were chosen by Jacobo Fitzjames Stuart, the publisher, and those in this edition by me).

There is a new section, new, at least, to this book (I did at one time include it in *Literatura y fantasma* [*Literature and Phantasm*], 1993), entitled "Fugitive Women," written after the 1992 publication of *Written Lives,* but very much in the same spirit, which is why this volume of brief biographies is the most suitable place for it. These pieces first saw the light in the magazine *Woman* (issues published May-October 1993).

As regards what I wrote in the Prologue seven years and seven months ago, the "conviction" I referred to then has become more widespread and more firmly established. And to my list of favourite Spanish authors I should now add—since he is no longer living—Juan Benet.

With the passage of time, I have come to realise that, although I have enjoyed writing all my books, this was the one with which I had the most fun. Perhaps because these "lives" were not just "written" but "read."

J.M.
September 1999

WILLIAM FAULKNER ON HORSEBACK

ACCORDING TO SOMEWHAT kitsch literary legend,
William Faulkner wrote his novel *As I Lay Dying* in the space of
six weeks and in the most precarious of situations, namely,
while he was working on the night shift down a mine, with the
pages resting on an upturned wheelbarrow and lit only by the
dim rays of the lamp affixed to his own dust-caked helmet. This
said kitsch legend is a clear attempt to enlist Faulkner in the
ranks of other poor, self-sacrificing, slightly proletarian writers.

The bit about the six weeks is the only true part: for six weeks one summer he made the most of the long, long intervals between feeding spadefuls of coal into the boiler he had been put in charge of in an electrical power plant. According to Faulkner, no one bothered him there, the continual hum from the enormous old dynamo was "soothing," and the place itself was otherwise "warm and silent."

There is certainly no doubting his ability to lose himself in his writing or his reading. His father had got him the position at the power station after he was dismissed from his previous job as a post office clerk at the University of Mississippi. Apparently one of the lecturers there, quite reasonably, complained: the only way he could get his letters was by rummaging around by the garbage can at the back door, where the unopened mail bags all too often ended up. Faulkner did not like having his reading interrupted, and the sale of stamps fell alarmingly: by way of explanation, Faulkner told his family that he was not prepared to keep getting up to wait on people at the window and having to be beholden to any son-of-a-bitch who had two cents to buy a stamp.

Perhaps that is where the seeds were first sown of Faulkner's evident aversion to and scorn for letters. When he died, piles of letters, packages and manuscripts sent by admirers were found, none of which he had opened. In fact, the only letters he did open were those from publishers, and then only very cautiously: he would make a tiny slit in the envelope and then shake it to see if a cheque appeared. If it didn't, then the letter would simply join all those other things that can wait forever.

He always had a keen interest in cheques, but one should not deduce from this that he was a greedy man or, indeed, mean. He was, in fact, something of a spendthrift. He got through any money he earned very quickly, then lived on credit for a while until the next cheque arrived. He would then pay his debts and start spending again, mostly on horses, cigarettes and whisky. He did not have many clothes, but those he had were expensive. When he was nineteen, his affected way of dressing earned him the nickname "The Count." If the fashion was for tight trousers, then his would be the tightest in the whole of Oxford (Mississippi), the town where he lived. He left there in 1916 to go to Toronto to train with the RAF. The Americans had rejected him because he didn't have enough qualifications, and the British didn't want him because he was too short, until, that is, he threatened to go and fly for the Germans instead.

On one occasion, a young man went to visit him and found him standing with his pipe, which had gone out, in one hand and, in the other, the bridle of the pony that his daughter Jill was riding. To break the ice, the young man asked if the little girl had been riding long. Faulkner did not reply at once. Then he said: "Three years," adding: "You know, a woman should know only how to do three things." He paused, then concluded: "Tell the truth, ride a horse, and sign a cheque."

Jill was not the first daughter Faulkner had with his wife, Estelle, who brought with her two children from a previous marriage. The first daughter they had together died only five days after being born. They called her Alabama. Her mother was still weak and in bed, and Faulkner's brothers were out of town at the time and never saw the child. Faulkner could see no point in holding a funeral, since in those five days the little girl had only had time to become a memory, not a person. So her father put her in a tiny coffin and carried her to the cemetery on his lap. Alone, he placed her in her grave, without telling anyone.

When he received the Nobel Prize in 1950, Faulkner was, at first, reluctant to go to Sweden. However, in the end, he not only went, he travelled throughout Europe and Asia on "a State

Department mission." He did not much enjoy the endless functions to which he was invited. At a party given in his honour by Gallimard, his French publishers, it is said that after each succinct reply to questions put by journalists, he would take a step backward. Step by step, he eventually found himself with his back to the wall, and only then did the journalists take pity on him or else give him up as a lost cause. He finally sought refuge in the garden. A few people decided to venture out there too, announcing that they were going to talk to Faulkner, only to come straight back in again, proffering excuses in faltering voices: "It's awfully cold out there." Faulkner was a taciturn man who loved silence, and went to the theatre only five times in his entire life: he had seen *Hamlet* three times, *A Midsummer Night's Dream,* and *Ben Hur,* and that was all. He had not read Freud either, at least so he said on one occasion: "I have never read him. Neither did Shakespeare. I doubt if Melville did either and I'm sure Moby Dick didn't." He read *Don Quixote* every year.

But then he also said that he never told the truth. After all, he wasn't a woman, although he did have a woman's love of cheques and horseback-riding. He always said that he had written *Sanctuary,* his most commercial novel, for money: "I needed it to buy a good horse." He also said that he didn't visit big cities very often because you couldn't go there on horseback. When he was getting older, against the advice of both his family and his doctors, he continued going out riding and jumping fences, and kept falling off. The last time he went riding he suffered just such a fall. From the house, his wife saw Faulkner's horse standing by the gate, with its saddle still on and the reins hanging loose. When she didn't see her husband there with the horse, she called Dr. Felix Linder and they went out looking for him. They found him over half a mile away, limping, almost dragging himself along. The horse had thrown him and he hadn't been able to remount, having fallen on his back. The horse

8

had walked on a few paces, then stopped and looked round. When Faulkner managed to get to his feet, the horse came over to him and touched him with its muzzle. Faulkner had tried to grab the reins, but failed. Then the horse had headed off towards the house.

William Faulkner spent some time in bed, badly injured and in great pain. He had still not fully recovered from the fall when he died. He was in the hospital, where he had been admitted for a check-up on his progress. But legend refuses to accept that the fall from his horse was the cause of his death. He was killed by a thrombosis on July 6, 1962, when he was not quite sixty-five.

When asked to name the best American writers of his day, he would say that they had all failed, but that Thomas Wolfe had been the finest failure and William Faulkner the second finest failure. He often repeated this over the years, but it is worth remembering that Thomas Wolfe had been dead since 1938, that is, during nearly all the years that Faulkner used to give this answer and was himself alive.

JOSEPH CONRAD ON LAND

JOSEPH CONRAD'S BOOKS about the sea are so many and so memorable that one always tends to think of him on board a sailing ship, forgetting that he spent the last thirty years of his existence on land, leading an unexpectedly sedentary life. In fact, like any good sailor, he hated travelling, and nothing consoled him more than being shut up in his study, writing with agonising difficulty or chatting with his closest friends. It has to be said, however, that he did not always work in rooms that were, in principle, intended for that purpose: towards the end of his life, he used to hide away in the most remote corners of the garden in his house in Kent, scribbling on scraps of paper, and once, it is said, he even annexed the bathroom for a whole week without a word of explanation to his family, who, during that time, enjoyed only very restricted use of that room. On another occasion, the problem was his clothes, for Conrad refused to wear anything but an extremely faded yellow-striped bathrobe, which proved most embarrassing when friends turned up unannounced or American tourists arrived, who claimed, oddly, to have just been passing by.

The gravest threat to family safety was, however, Conrad's deep-rooted need to have a cigarette clamped between his fingers at all times, although this was usually only for a matter of seconds, since he would immediately put it down somewhere and forget about it. His wife, Jessie, resigned herself to the fact that books, sheets, tablecloths, and furniture were all covered in burn marks, but she lived for years in a state of high alert lest her husband burn himself, for even when he gave in to her pleas and got into the habit of throwing his cigarette butts into a large jug of water placed there for that purpose, he had constant incendiary mishaps. On more than one occasion, his clothes nearly got scorched when he sat too close to a stove, and it was not unusual for the book he was reading suddenly to catch fire after prolonged contact with the candle illuminating it.

Conrad was, needless to say, absentminded, but while his main characteristics—irritability and deference—may seem contradictory, they can, perhaps, be explained reciprocally. His natural state was one of disquiet bordering on anxiety, and such was his concern for others that the slightest setback suffered by one of his friends would provoke in him an attack of gout, an illness he had contracted as a young man in the Malay Archipelago and which tormented him for the rest of his life.

When his son, Borys, was fighting in the First World War, his wife returned home one night, having been away all day, and was received by a tearful maid who told her that Mr. Conrad had informed the servants that Borys had been killed and had, since then, been closeted in their son's room. And yet, added the maid, no letter or telegram had arrived. When Jessie George Conrad, legs shaking, went upstairs to find her distraught husband and ask him how he could be so sure, he replied, offended: "Can't I have a presentiment as well as you? I *know* he has been killed!" Presently, Conrad grew a little calmer and fell asleep. His presentiment proved false, but, it seems, once his imagination was let loose, there was no stopping it. He lived in a permanent state of extreme tension, and that was the source of his irritability, which he could barely control and yet which, once it had passed, left neither trace nor memory. When his wife was giving birth to their first son, the aforementioned Borys, Conrad was pacing anxiously up and down in the garden. Suddenly he heard a child cry and strode indignantly over to the kitchen to tell the maid: "Send that child away at once; it will disturb Mrs. Conrad!" Apparently the maid shouted back at him even more indignantly: "It's your own child, sir!"

Conrad was so irritable that whenever he dropped his pen, instead of picking it up at once and carrying on writing, he would spend several minutes exasperatedly drumming his fingers on the desk as if bemoaning what had occurred. His character remained an enigma to those around him. His inner state of agitation would sometimes cause him to fall silent for long periods, even in the company of his friends, who would wait patiently until he resumed the conversation, in which, ordinarily, he was extremely animated, displaying a remarkable gift for story-telling. They say that his tone then was more like the tone in his book of essays, *The Mirror of the Sea*, than in his stories or novels. After one of these interminable and apparently ruminative silences, he would usually come out with some unlikely question that had nothing whatsoever to do with what they had been talking about up until then, for example: "What do you think of Mussolini?"

Conrad wore a monocle and disliked poetry. According to his wife, he only ever gave his approval to two books of verse, one by a young Frenchman whose name she could not recall and the other by his friend Arthur Symons. There are, however, those who maintain that he liked Keats and hated Shelley. The author he hated most, though, was Dostoyevsky. He hated him because he was Russian, because he was mad, and because he was confused, and the mere mention of his name would provoke a furious outburst. He devoured books, with Flaubert and Maupassant heading the list of those he most admired, and took such pleasure in prose that, long before proposing to the woman who would become his wife (that is, when they were still not as yet close companions), he turned up one night bearing a bundle of papers and suggested that the young woman read a few of these pages—part of his second novel—out loud. Full of fear and trembling, Jessie George obeyed, but Conrad's own nervousness did not help: "Never mind that part," he would say. "That is not going to stand—never mind it—start three lines lower; over leaf, over leaf." He even criticised her diction: "Speak distinctly; if you're tired, say so; don't eat your words. You English are all alike, you make the same sound for every letter." The odd thing is that this same persnickety Conrad had, until the end of his days, an extremely thick foreign accent in the language which, as a writer, he came to master better than any author of his day.

Conrad did not get married until he was thirty-eight and when he finally made his proposal, after they had known each other and been friends for several years, it proved to be as pessimistic as some of his own stories, for he announced that he did not have very long to live and had absolutely no intention of having children. The optimistic part came afterwards and consisted in him adding that, such as his life was, he thought that he and Jessie might spend a few happy years together. The bride-to-be's mother commented that: "she didn't quite see why he wished to get married." Conrad, nevertheless, was a devoted husband: he often brought his wife flowers and, each time he finished a book, he would make her some generous gift.

Despite having lost his parents at an early age and despite preserving few memories of them, he was a man much preoccupied with family tradition and with his forebears, even going so far as to express his repeated regret that a great-uncle of his, retreating with Napoleon from Moscow, had been so hard pressed by hunger that he was forced to find temporary respite from it, along with one or two other officers, at the expense of "a luckless Lithuanian dog." The fact that a relative of his should have consumed dog-meat seemed to him a disgrace, and one for which, moreover, he held Bonaparte himself indirectly to blame.

Conrad died quite suddenly, on August 3, 1924, at his house in Kent, at the age of sixty-six. He had felt unwell the previous day, but nothing suggested that death was imminent. That is why, when death came, he was alone in his room, resting. His wife, who was in the room next door, heard him shout: "Here...!", followed by a second stifled word that she could not make out, and then a noise. Conrad had slipped out of his chair onto the floor.

Just as he would have liked to erase his great-uncle's Lithuanian escapade, Conrad would, in later life, occasionally deny that he had written certain pieces (articles, stories, chapters written in collaboration with Ford Madox Ford) which were undoubtedly his and had even been published under his name. He would, nonetheless, deny them and claim that he could not remember them. And when he was shown manuscripts and it was proven to him that the pages in question had undeniably come from his pen, he would simply shrug his shoulders, one of his most characteristic gestures, and lapse into one of his silences. All those who met him agree that he was a man of great irony, but an irony of a kind that his acquired English compatriots did not always catch, or which, perhaps, they did not understand.

Isak Dinesen in Old Age

THE TRUE IMAGE of Isak Dinesen was, for a long time, that of a ghostly old lady, elegant and deeply enigmatic, until the cinema replaced it with the excessively romantic and rather drippy image of a long-suffering, colonial aristocrat. Not that Baroness Blixen did not have a tendency toward the romantic and the aristocratic, but it would be fairer to say that she played at it, at least she did once she became Isak Dinesen, that is, once she began to be published under that and other names, and returned to Denmark after her long, unsuccessful years in Africa. "We wear masks as we grow older, the masks of our age, and the young… think that we are the way we look. But that is not the case."

When, in 1959, she made her first visit to America, the country where her books had achieved the most success and been received with most interest, she was preceded by endless rumours and mysteries: she is, in fact, a man; he is, in fact, a woman; Isak Dinesen is actually two people, brother and sister; Isak Dinesen lived in Boston in 1870; she's from Paris really; he lives in Elsinore; she spends most of her time in London; she's a nun; he's very hospitable and welcomes young writers as his guests; she's rarely seen and lives like a recluse; she writes in French; no, in English; no, in Danish; no, in… When she finally made her appearance at the numerous parties to which she was invited and at the packed public readings where she told her stories entirely without the aid of notes, they discovered that she was a frail, eccentric old lady, deeply lined and with matchstick-thin arms, all dressed in black, with a turban on her head, diamonds in her ears and large amounts of kohl around her eyes. Despite this, the legend continued, albeit along more concrete lines: according to the Americans, she lived on a diet of oysters and champagne, which was not quite true, for she also consumed prawns, asparagus, grapes, and tea. When Isak Dinesen expressed a desire to meet Marilyn Monroe, the novelist Carson McCullers managed to arrange this, and, at a famous lunch, the three women shared a table with Arthur Miller, the husband par excellence, who, surprised by the Baroness's eating habits, asked which doctor had prescribed this diet of oysters and champagne. They say that America has never seen the like of the scornful look she gave him: "Doctor?" she said. "The doctors are horrified, but I love champagne and I love oysters and they do me good." Miller went on to make some comment about protein, and it seems that the second scornful look she gave him will also never be seen again on American soil: "I don't know anything about that," came her reply, "I am an old woman and I eat what agrees with me." The Baroness got on much better with Marilyn Monroe.

The truth is that Isak Dinesen lived mainly at Rungstedlund, her childhood home in Denmark, and was obliged to lead a very sedentary life due to her many ailments, the most enduring of which had nothing at all to do with age but with the syphilis she had contracted after a year of marriage to Baron Bror Blixen, who, after much vacillation, she eventually divorced. This husband was the twin brother of the man she had loved from girlhood, and bonds formed through a third party are perhaps the most difficult to break.

Having syphilis obliged her, early on, to renounce sex, and seeing that there was no help to be had from God and bearing in mind how terrible it was for a young woman to be denied "the right to love," Isak Dinesen promised her soul to the Devil, and he promised her, in return, that everything she experienced thenceforth would become a story. That, at least, is what she told a non-lover—she was twice his age and three times as intelligent—the Danish poet Thorkild Bjørnvig, with whom she made a strange pact when she was sixty-four and whom she dominated and kept in a state of complete subjugation for four years. She enjoyed frightening this non-lover with her abrupt changes of mood, her calculated surprises, her charm, and her disconcerting but always persuasive views. On one occasion, she startled him with this explanation of the nature of her being: "You are better than I am, that is the problem," she told him. "The difference between us is that you have an immortal soul and I do not. It is the same with mermaids and water sprites, they do not have one either. They live longer than those with immortal souls, but when they die, they disappear totally and without a trace. But who can entertain and please and transport people better than a water sprite when she is present, when she plays and enchants and makes people dance more wildly and love more ardently than they normally do? She will disappear and all that she will leave behind is a streak of water along the floor."

When this poet (whom she urged to leave both wife and child in order to spend long periods "creating" in her house in Rungstedlund) proved inadequate to the task (as was nearly always the case), the Baroness would grow angry and mistreat him, as she would when he dared to express any reservations about her own writings. But Isak Dinesen was never constant and, after some enormous row, she was capable of behaving perfectly charmingly at their next meeting, as if nothing had happened, even congratulating her non-lover on his incorruptible critical sense. Such transformations were typical of her, and the poet Bjørnvig tells how, one night, for reasons that escaped even him, Isak Dinesen flew into a rage and was transformed into a decrepit, gesticulating fury, shrivelled up with anger, leaving him feeling wretched and paralysed. Afterwards, when the poet had returned to his room, the Baroness slipped in and sat down on the edge of his bed: now, however, she looked radiant, transfigured, as lovely as a seventeen-year-old. Björnvig confessed that had he not personally witnessed the transformation, he himself would not have believed it possible.

The Baroness also provided this non-lover and her friends with moments of enormous pleasure, enchantment and reverie. On one occasion, and in the middle of a delightful evening, she got up and left the room. She came back a little later carrying a revolver, which she held levelled at Björnvig for quite some time. According to him, he was not in the least taken aback by this because, in the state of perfect happiness in which he found himself, death would not have mattered. Needless to say, Bjørnvig did not publish anything during the four years that this rapture lasted.

Isak Dinesen claimed to have poor sight, yet she could spot a four-leaf clover in a field from a remarkable distance away, and could see the new moon when it was not yet visible. When she saw it, she would curtsy to it three times, and, she claimed, you must never look at it through glass, because that spelled bad luck. She played the piano and the flute, preferably Schubert on the first and Handel on the second, and in the evenings, she would often recite poems by her favourite poet, Heine, and sometimes by Goethe, whom she detested, but nevertheless recited. She loathed Dostoyevsky, although she admired him too, and was a stalwart of Shakespeare. She would frequently quote these lines by Heine: "You wanted to be happy, infinitely happy or infinitely wretched, proud heart, and now you are wretched."

According to those who looked into them, her kohl-lined eyes were full of secrets; they never blinked and remained fixed on whatever they were looking at. Isak Dinesen's father had committed suicide when she was ten years old, and she had told stories ever since she was a child. Her younger sister as she climbed wearily into bed would sometimes plead with her: "Oh, Tania, not tonight!" In her old age, on the other hand, her hosts or her guests would beg her to tell them stories. She would occasionally oblige, like someone making a gift. Every Thursday, she would have supper in the company of a little boy for whom she had purchased a suit appropriate for the occasion: he was the son of her cook, and she had discovered him one night spying on her while she dined alone. She liked to be provocative, but always in a gentle and ironic way, as when she expressed doubts about absolute democracy, fearing for the fate of the elite: "There should always be a few who are versed in the classics." She claimed to live her life according to the rules of classical tragedy and would have brought up the children she never had to do the same.

In the end, she spent several months of each year in a clinic, and the rest, as always, at Rungstedlund, where she died peacefully on September 7, 1962, having listened to Brahms during the evening. She smoked incessantly until the end of her life, which she departed at the age of seventy-seven, and was buried at the foot of a beech tree she herself had chosen, on the Rungsted coast. According to Lawrence Durrell, she would have shot a fond, ironic glance at anyone daring to mourn her death. "I am, in fact, three thousand years old and have dined with Socrates."

Isak Dinesen made these words her own: "There is no mystery in art. Do the things you can see, they will show you what you cannot see."

JAMES JOYCE IN HIS POSES

PEOPLE USED TO SAY of James Joyce that he seemed sad and tired, and he described himself on one occasion as "a jealous, lonely, dissatisfied, proud man." This description was, of course, given in private, in a letter to his wife, Nora Barnacle, to whom he confided far more intimate and daring things than he did to any other person. Not that one should deduce from this that he did not also intend the description for posterity, to which he confided still more daring things.

As a young man, he was already rather pompous and full of himself, concerned only with what he would write and with his early (and, later, perennial) hatred of Ireland and the Irish. When he had still written only a few poems, he asked his brother Stanislaus: "Don't you think there is a certain resemblance between the mystery of the Mass and what I am trying to do? I mean that I am trying in my poems to give people some kind of intellectual pleasure or spiritual enjoyment by converting the bread of daily life into something that has a permanent artistic life of its own…for their mental, moral, and spiritual uplift." When he was older his comparisons may have been less eucharistic and more modest, but he was always convinced of the extreme importance of his work, even before it existed. James Joyce appears to have been one of those artists who so ostentatiously adopt the pose of genius that they end up persuading their contemporaries and several generations more that they not only are geniuses, but that they always—indubitably and irremissibly—were. In keeping with this pose, he was famous because he did not care whether people read him or not, nor, of course, what they thought of him; yet, when *Ulysses* came out—after enormous difficulties finding a publisher—he did all he could to promote it and was even occasionally seen wrapping up a copy for a customer in the famous bookshop Shakespeare & Co., under whose seal and impress the immortal book was finally published. It is also known that he waited, alert and expectant, for any mention or review in the press and wrote courteous thank-you notes to anyone who took an interest in the novel. When, much later, the publication of *Finnegans Wake* received a cool reception, he felt hurt and unhappy, and spent the last two years of his life nursing these feelings, which is not a pleasant way to spend one's years, especially when they are one's last.

For nearly all the other years of his life, however, he

enjoyed a degree of respect and admiration which few authors achieve before death. During the time he spent in Paris, he was both revered and feared, and no one ever opposed his wishes or his habits, for example, dining every night in the same place and at nine o'clock sharp, or never drinking white wine, however good it might be. Apparently, an oculist had assured him that white wine was ruinous to the eyesight, and Joyce took great care of his delicate eyes. Threatened by glaucoma, he had to undergo eleven operations during his lifetime, which is why some photographs show him wearing a large and very obvious eye patch, and this is perhaps also why Djuna Barnes saw in his eyes "the same paleness seen in plants long hidden from the sun." He did not, therefore, wear it in order to be noticed: Joyce's pose as genius was quite sufficient, and he did not need to disguise himself as a hunter or to run with the bulls in Pamplona. On the contrary, he was far from flamboyant, and to have to sit by his side at a supper or a social gathering was agony, at least for anyone even moderately talkative, since, in these circumstances, Joyce would not deign to open his mouth, but expected to be kept entertained with chatter while he remained silent, "an easy but absolute silence" in the words of Ford Madox Ford. His fellow diners would struggle to come up with subjects that might interest him, but Mr. Joyce (everyone but Djuna Barnes called him that) would reply only with a "Yes" or a "No." Unlike the characters in his novels, all of whom were interior gasbags, the author was always taciturn and disdainful, at least in society.

In private and alone, he was very different, although no less haughty. He would drink until well into the small hours and was friendlier and more talkative, although he did, all too often, propose theological subjects that were of no interest to anyone else, or would begin reciting, in sonorous Italian, whole chunks of Dante, like a priest before his congregation. On one occasion, in the Brasserie Lutétia, his companion mentioned that he had seen a rat running down the stairs, and Joyce's reaction was anything but serene. "Where? Where?" he asked in alarm. "That's bad luck." Joyce was highly superstitious, and a second after uttering these words, he fainted in terror. He was also very afraid of dogs, having been badly bitten as a child by an Irish terrier. What terrified him most, though, both in childhood and adulthood, were storms, although, as an adult, he was better able to disguise this. As a child, it wasn't enough to close windows, draw curtains, and pull down the blinds, he had to shut himself up in a closet. According to malicious tongues, even as a grown man, he used to clap his hands over his ears and behave in a most cowardly manner; kinder tongues deny this and say only that if he was out in the street during a storm, he would wring his hands, scream and run.

As well as being a heavy drinker when he drank (for he had periods of abstinence too), he was a great devourer of books and had, in his youth, been a frequenter of prostitutes. Although he used to go with prostitutes, he did not like them, which is perhaps why, when he wrote to his wife, Nora, he chose to imagine scenes which, for all their theatricality, may well have borne some relation to reality. Joyce had, after all, once said that he "longed to copulate with a soul." These obscene letters achieved notoriety some years ago, and in them the author expressed his high hopes for the day he and Nora would be together again (he was in Dublin and she in Trieste, where they usually lived), and in them he even found some momentary happiness, given that at the end of more than one letter he confesses that he came (his words) while he was writing her this filth: he is doubtless one of the few writers to have achieved such intense gratification with his pen. To judge by this correspondence, James Joyce wanted his wife to put on weight so that she could beat him and dominate him and practise other excesses, and he had very precise ideas about what undergarments she should wear (his invariable preference was that they should be slightly soiled) and showed a clear predilection for the aerial or even depository capabilities of the woman he had met as Nora Barnacle; in short, he was a coprophiliac. This, however, is not the most lurid aspect of the letters, but, rather, the inquisitive spirit in which he interrogates Nora about her past and her present, in order to feed his books. The interrogation resembles, more than anything, that of a Catholic priest in the confessional, as one can see from this extract: "When that person... put his hand or hands under your skirts, did he only tickle you outside or did he put his finger or fingers up into you? If he did, did they go up far enough to touch that little cock at the end of your cunt? Did he touch you behind? Did he ask you to touch him and did you do so? If you did not touch him did he come against you and did you feel it?" Or in another letter: "Tonight...I have been trying to picture you frigging your cunt in the closet. How do you do it? Do you stand against the wall with your hand tickling up under your clothes or do you squat down on the hole with your skirts up and your hand hard at work in through the slit of your drawers? Does it give you the horn now to shit? I wonder how you can do it. Do you come in the act of shitting or do you frig yourself off first and then shit?" No one can deny that Joyce was a scrupulous man with a love of detail.

James Joyce suffered various misfortunes in his life, but, generally speaking, he did not show his feelings. Five of his nine brothers and sisters (he was the oldest) died as children, and his response to these deaths made even his mother think him heartless. On the other hand, when his daughter Lucia had to be admitted to various psychiatric hospitals, Joyce was all solicitude and never lost hope of her recovery. He wrote her numerous letters. According to his brother Stanislaus, however, for James Joyce "unhappiness was like a vice." He was cold and distant except with those closest to him, but when, on his mother's death, he discovered a bundle of letters that his father had written to her before they were married, he spent the whole afternoon reading them "with as little compunction as a doctor or a lawyer… puts questions." When he had finished, Stanislaus asked him: "Well?" "Nothing," James Joyce answered curtly and rather contemptuously. Nothing, thought Stanislaus, for the young poet with a mission, but clearly something for the woman who had kept them through all those years of neglect and poverty. Stanislaus burned them, without reading them himself.

James Joyce had a habit of sighing. Another mother, his wife Nora's, noticed this and said that he would destroy his heart by doing this. Joyce, however, did not die from a heart destroyed by grief, but from a perforated ulcer, in a hospital in Zurich, on January 13, 1941, when he was almost fifty-nine. They buried him two days later, after a brief ceremony, in the cemetery of that city.

His own wife, Nora Barnacle, who never bothered to read *Ulysses*, once summed him up. She said: "He's a fanatic."

Giuseppe Tomasi di Lampedusa in Class

THE SADDEST THING about the whole rather sad story of
Giuseppe Tomasi di Lampedusa is the publication of his one
world-famous novel *The Leopard*, because it could be said that it
was the only extraordinary thing to have happened in his life,
and even that happened, in fact, in death, sixteen months after
he had departed this world. This is why he is one of the few
writers who never felt he was a writer or lived as if he were one,
even less so than others who also failed to publish anything dur-

ing their lifetime, for the simple reason that he did not even attempt to do so until almost the end of his days. Not only did he make no attempt to get published, he hardly even attempted to write.

He was more of a *reader*, insatiable and obsessive. The few people who knew him well were astonished at his encyclopaedic knowledge of literature and history, on both of which subjects he possessed a vast library. He had not only read all the important and essential writers, but also the second-rate and the mediocre, whom, especially as regards the novel, he considered to be as necessary as the great: "One has to learn how to be bored," he used to say, and he read bad literature with interest and patience. Buying books was almost his sole expense and sole luxury, although the possibilities that Palermo offered in this respect to a man who knew English, French, German and Russian (as well as Spanish in the last year of his life) were desperately limited. Nevertheless, given the futile existence he led, that of a provincial aristocrat, he would spend at least a couple of hours each morning inspecting the bookshops, especially one called Flaccovio, which he visited every day for ten years.

The truth is that Lampedusa's mornings must have appeared to his fellow citizens to be mornings of utter idleness, which they doubtless were. While Licy, his Latvian psychoanalyst wife, recovered in bed from the hours which, by her own choosing, she spent working late into the night, Lampedusa would get up early and walk to a café-cum-patisserie where he would take a long breakfast and read. On one occasion, he did not move for four hours, the time it took him to finish a large novel by Balzac, from start to finish. Then he would undertake his long tour of the bookshops, after which he would go to another café where he would sit but not mix with a few acquaintances of his with semi-intellectual pretensions. He would listen (to "their nonsense") and hardly say a word, then, after all these marathon sittings and feeble peregrinations, return home on the bus. He is always described as walking wearily along, looking very distinguished, but with a somewhat careless gait, his eyes alert and holding in his hand a leather bag crammed with the books and cakes and biscuits on which he would have to survive until evening, since lunch was never served at home. He carried that famous bag with great nonchalance, quite unconcerned that volumes of Proust should be sitting cheek by jowl with titbits and even courgettes. Apparently the bag always contained more books than were strictly necessary, as if it were the luggage of a reader setting off on a long journey, who was afraid he might run out of reading matter while away. According to his wife, he always had some Shakespeare with him, so that "he could console himself with it if he should see something disagreeable" on his wanderings.

So passionate was Lampedusa's love of books that he even used them as strongboxes: he was in the habit of placing small quantities of money between the pages of various volumes, always forgetting afterwards, of course, in which book those notes were to be found. This was the basis for his remark that his library contained two different kinds of treasure.

Money, as you can imagine, never constituted a problem for him, but less because he was very rich than because he lacked all ambition. While it is true that he was wealthy enough never to have to work, a shared inheritance and the various crises of the century made of him very much a nobleman come down in the world. His habits were modest: apart from bookshops, these consisted in frequent visits to the cinema and occasional meals out at a restaurant; he did not even travel, although he had done so fairly often in his youth. He noted down in his diary which films he had seen (two or three a week), along with a single adjective: when he saw *20,000 Leagues Under the Sea*, the adjective he chose was *spettacolare*.

In 1954, three years before his death, he wrote: "I am a very solitary person. Out of the sixteen hours I spend awake each day, at least ten are spent in solitude. I do not, however, spend all that time reading; sometimes I amuse myself by concocting literary theories..." This is not entirely true, since, after his death, he did not leave behind him anything that could be described as literary theory. What he did leave were about a thousand pages on English and French literature, and the astonishing thing is that, initially, these pages were intended for just one person, Francesco Orlando. He was a young man from a bourgeois family (and now an illustrious teacher and critic) to whom Lampedusa, in his final years, offered to teach both English and a complete course on the literature of that language. Occasionally, that only student was not alone, but this was very much the exception. Three times a week, at six o'clock in the evening, Lampedusa would receive Orlando in his house and have him slowly read out the lesson that he, the prince, had written for this purpose, or else they would read together, especially Dickens and Shakespeare. This generous, selfless and idiosyncratic method of teaching changed Lampedusa's life, and in it may lie, in part, the origin of his belated decision to write. At any rate, this contact with young people and the chance to "transmit something to them" (the literary talks, if not the classes, spread to other friends the same age as Orlando) revitalised him and filled his evenings with something more than mere solitary reading. He took these classes very seriously indeed, as evidenced by comments he made bemoaning their bad or hasty preparation: "the worst pages ever written by human pen," is how he described what he had written on the life of Byron, "an utter abomination." His gentle irony led his pupil to believe that, once read by him and, indeed, as soon as he left the house, the fate of these texts was to be consigned immediately to the fire. Fortunately, however, Lampedusa kept them, and these pages—not at all scholarly, but full of wisdom, humour, seriousness and refinement—are now beginning to be published.

He was very interested in writers' lives, believing, like Sainte-Beuve, that in those lives, or in their most secret anecdotes, could be found the key to a writer's work. Perhaps that is why—as well as making the work of exegetes more difficult— he left very few anecdotes himself, and if there were secrets in his life, he did his best to ensure that they remained so (that is, he kept them secret). The only scrap of gossip about Lampedusa, of the kind he liked to know about his idols, was that he may have been impotent, as suggested by the fact that he had no children (but then he was thirty-seven when he married his wife) and by his apparent lack of passion for Licy, with whom, in the early years, when she found Sicily hard to bear and spent a large part of the year at the palace in Latvia where she had been born, he kept up what has been called *un matrimonio epistolare*—"an epistolary marriage." Any other anomalies belonged not to him, but to his ancestors, the closest being the murder of an aunt of his, stabbed to death in a seedy Roman hotel by the baron who was her lover.

Lampedusa was as eccentric and obsessive as all writers, even though he did not know he was a writer: he hated melodrama and Italian opera, which he considered a barbarous art; in fact, he hated anything explicit. His favourite Shakespeare play was *Measure for Measure*, but he preferred, above all, Sonnet 129. He suffered from insomnia and from nightmares, but only at the end of his life did he deign to recount one of these to his psychoanalyst wife: in the dream he was walking down corridors asking for information about his imminent execution. He drank only water, but he ate well (he was plump) and smoked heavily, not even noticing the ash sprinkling his jacket. He would shake the hand of the person being introduced to him without looking the person in the face; in society, he was shy, taciturn, solitary and sad, so much so that many people believed that, in certain circumstances, he simply refused to speak. In private, on the other hand, with his few close friends and even fewer pupils, his conversation was brilliant and precise, pleasant and always slightly sarcastic. He could be pedantic: he spoke to each of his dogs in one of the various languages he knew. Francesco Orlando said of him that he had the air of "a vast, abstracted feline."

Little is known about his political views, if, indeed, he had any very clear views, apart from his hatred of Sicily and the Sicilians, although this was a superficial hatred, for it carried with it a large dash of love. But he condemned all of Sicily's social classes. He was anticlerical, in the old-fashioned way, and believed, anyway, that everything ended "down here." Gentle in manner, he accepted with irony and sorrow the initial rejection of his novel by some publishing houses, while his wife noted eloquently in her diary: "*Refus de ce cochon de Mondadori*" ("Rejected by that pig from Mondadori"). According to Lampedusa, what finally made him decide to write was seeing one of his cousins, Lucio Piccolo, another late starter, win both a prize and the applause of Montale for a volume of poems he had written. "Being mathematically certain that I was no more foolish than Lucio, I sat down at my desk and wrote a novel," he said in a letter to a friend. He was convinced that *The Leopard* deserved to see the light of day, but he also had his doubts: "It is, I fear, rubbish," he remarked to Francesco Orlando, who claims that he said this in good faith.

Giuseppe Tomasi di Lampedusa died of lung cancer on the morning of July 23, 1957, at the age of sixty, at the house of some relatives in Rome, where he had gone for treatment. He was sleeping, and his sister-in-law found him.

Lampedusa believed that one always had to leave people to

make their own mistakes. He, of course, made his, and knew nothing of the success that chose not to hurry for him. One of the misfortunes of his life, he said, had been a certain hardness of heart, and he once gave this warning to his beloved cousin Gioacchino, who was forty years his junior and whom Lampedusa finally adopted: "Be careful," he said. "*Cave obdurationem cordis.*"

Henry James on a Visit

IT CAN BE SAID of Henry James that he was made both
miserable and happy by the same thing, namely, that he was a
mere spectator who barely participated in life, or, at least, not in
its most striking and exciting aspects. On the other hand, he led,
for many years, the most intense and demanding of social lives,
so much so that in one season alone, 1878-79, he received (and
accepted) precisely one hundred and forty dinner invitations.

This was the era when no first night or party was blighted by his absence.

He spent the greater part of the last eighteen years of his life, however, at Lamb House, his country residence in Rye, not that he exactly lacked for company there either: to his four servants, gardener and secretary were added numerous visitors throughout the seasons, albeit in orderly and unpromiscuous fashion, for he never had more than two guests at a time. Nearby lived a few fellow writers, such as Joseph Conrad and Ford Madox Ford, whose surname at the time was still Hueffer. James had little to do with the first of these, because, although he admired his work, he remained dissatisfied with the man, mainly because "at bottom" he was a Pole, a Roman Catholic, a Romantic, and a Slav pessimist. However, when they did meet, they spoke with great ceremony and admiration and always in French; every thirty seconds James would exclaim *"Mon cher confrère!"* to which Conrad would respond with equal frequency *"Mon cher maître!"* As for Ford or Hueffer, who was much younger than James, they saw each other almost constantly according to the former, but this may have been rather more often than James wanted: there is objective evidence that, on one occasion, when out with his secretary, James jumped over a ditch in order to avoid an encounter on the road to Rye, where Hueffer used to wait for him to pass.

Henry James was a large man, verging on the obese, completely bald and with terrifying eyes, so penetrating and intelligent that the servants of some of the houses he visited would tremble when they opened the door to him, convinced that they were being pierced through to the very backbone. His bald head made him look like a theologian and his eyes like a wizard. And yet he was always highly circumspect and slightly humorous in his dealings with other people, as if he were deliberately imitating Pickwick. If something bothered him, though, he could be unbelievably cruel and momentarily vindictive, albeit only verbally. Those close to him remember that only rarely did his English become brutal and direct, but they never forgot those few occasions. On the whole, he spoke as he wrote, which sometimes led him to exasperating extremes, exacerbated by his habit, during his final years, of dictating his novels. The simplest question addressed to a servant would take a minimum of three minutes to formulate, such was his linguistic punctiliousness and his horror of inexactitude and error. In his zeal for clarity, his speech became utterly oblique and obscure, and, on one occasion, when referring to a dog, and wishing to avoid the actual word, he ended up defining it as "something black, something canine." He found himself equally unable to declare that an actress was frankly ugly, and had to make do with saying that "one of the poor wantons had a certain cadaverous grace."

He spoke with so many interpolations and parentheses that this occasionally got him into difficulties: one afternoon, he went out for a walk along the Rye road, as was his custom, with Hueffer and another writer and with his dog Maximilian, who liked to chase sheep and who was, for this reason, kept on a leash, but one long enough to allow him considerable freedom of movement. At one point, in order to conclude one particularly immense sentence with due emphasis, James stopped and planted his walking stick firmly in the ground, and in that position held forth for a long time while his companions listened in reverential silence, and the dog Maximilian, running about, back and forth, as the fancy took him, wound his leash around the walking stick and the gentlemen's legs, leaving them trapped. The Master finished his speech and wanted to continue on his way, but found himself immobilised. When he did, with some difficulty, extricate himself, he turned, eyes blazing, to Hueffer, reproachfully brandished his walking stick and cried: "Hueffer! You are painfully young, but at no more than the age to which you have attained, the playing of such tricks is an imbecility! An im... be... cility!"

Apart from these rare fits of rage, James was renowned for his impeccable manners and for never putting a foot wrong. He spoke with the same urbanity and—always—in the same circumlocutory fashion to diplomats and chimney sweeps, and felt infinite curiosity about whatever happened to pass before his eyes. Perhaps that is why he invited confidence, and, while in Rye, he certainly never scorned village gossip. He listened ceaselessly and talked ceaselessly too: he even heard the confession of a murderer and once gave a lecture on hats to Conrad's five-year-old son, who had, in all innocence, asked him about the unusual shape of the hat James himself was wearing.

When he was immersed in one of his novels, he could be very forgetful and it would entirely slip his mind that he had guests for lunch until they were there waiting for him, sitting round the table, but he was extremely careful and exacting when it came to the rules of hospitality, which is why, with him, the real danger lay not in being his guest, but his host, for he would draw definitive conclusions, which his imagination would subsequently embellish, based entirely on the attentions he had received or on the atmosphere of a house. Thus, for example, while he admired Turgenev both as a writer and a man (he viewed him as little less than a prince), he always hated Flaubert for having once received himself and Turgenev in his dressing gown. It was, it seems, more like some sort of work garment, known in French at the time as a *chandail*, and this was probably Flaubert's way of honouring them and admitting them into the privacy of his home. For James, however, it was indubitably a dressing gown and he never forgave him: indeed, Flaubert became for him a man who did *everything* in a dressing gown, and his books were consequently deemed to be failures, apart from *Madame Bovary*, which James conceded might have been written while Flaubert was wearing a waistcoat. Exactly the same mistake was made by the poet and painter Rossetti, who received him in his painting garb, which, for James, was tantamount to receiving him in a dressing gown. And to receive someone thus was a dishonor that revealed the soul of the perpetrator: this fact led James to infer that Rossetti had disgusting habits, never took baths and was insupportably lecherous. He probably breakfasted on greasy ham and undercooked eggs. Equally lacking in cordiality was an encounter with Oscar Wilde, whom he met in America where the aesthetic apostle was staying. When James happened to mention that he was missing London, Wilde looked at him scornfully and called him provincial, saying: "Really! You care for *places!*" And he added tritely: "The world is my home!" From then on, James referred to him variously as "an unclean beast," "a fatuous fool," or "a tenth-rate cad." On the other hand, his enthusiasm for Maupassant knew no bounds, again thanks to a single visit: the French short-story writer had received him for lunch in the society of a lady who was not only naked, but wearing a mask. This struck James as the height of refinement, especially when Maupassant informed him that she was no mere courtesan, prostitute, servant, or actress, but a *femme du monde*, which James was perfectly happy to believe.

As everyone knows, his relationships with women, for whatever reason, and several have been suggested, were well-nigh non-existent. Sex, however, does not appear to have been a matter of complete indifference to him, even though there is almost no explicit reference to it in his books, for when alone with certain people, he thought nothing of enquiring shamelessly and without recourse to euphemism about the most tortuous of sexual aberrations. For many years, he made it clear that he would never marry: on the one hand, and despite having lived in England for forty years, he thought the idea of taking a British wife ridiculous; on the other hand, as he said to a friend when discussing marriage: "I am both happy and miserable enough, as it is, and don't wish to add to either side of the account." According to him, marriage was not a necessity, but the ultimate and most expensive of luxuries. Women had, it appears, given him a few griefs and heartaches. On one occasion, he described to a friend, in serious and enigmatic fashion, how, in his youth, in a foreign city, he had stood for hours in the rain keeping watch on a window, waiting for a figure to appear, or perhaps a face left unlit by the lamp that gleamed for a second and was then extinguished for ever. "That was the end...," said James, and broke off. And when Hueffer announced that he was going to America and would be visiting Newport, Rhode Island, James asked him to take a stroll to a particular cliff and there render homage, on his behalf, to the place where he had seen for the last time and bade farewell to his now dead cousin who, when he was a very young man, he should have married.

Those who knew him remember him as a bright, alert man, restless, nervous, gesticulating and, at the same time, slow and deliberate. He was prudent in whatever he said or did, but not cautious; that is, he found it hard to resolve to do something, but once he did—for example when he was writing—he was unstoppable. While he was dictating his books, he would pace up and down, and when he ate alone, he would often leave the table and pace the dining room as he chewed his food. He very much liked being driven in a car and erroneously believed that he knew the area well and was blessed with an excellent sense of direction, which led him and the indulgent owners of various cars to arrive late and exhausted at their destinations, having taken endless and unnecessary detours under the guidance of Henry James. He almost never spoke about his own works, but lavished great care on his library, which he himself dusted with a silk handkerchief. He did not understand why his books did not sell better than they did, although *Daisy Miller* was very nearly a best-seller. His friend Edith Wharton once asked their joint publisher to pay her far larger royalties into James's account. James never found out.

Henry James died on the evening of February 28, 1916, at the age of seventy-two, after a long illness during which he suffered attacks of delirium: one day he dictated two letters as if he were Napoleon, one of them addressed to his brother Joseph Bonaparte, urging him to accept the throne of Spain. Months before, on recovering from the first such attack, he had been able to describe how, when he fell to the floor convinced that he was dying, he had heard in the room a voice not his own saying: "So it has come at last—the Distinguished Thing!"

Arthur Conan Doyle and Women

IT SEEMS IMPLAUSIBLE that a man as irreproachable and well-loved as Arthur Conan Doyle could, at the end of his days, have lost much of his reputation and even the respect of many of his friends. Yet this is precisely what happened when, eleven years before his death, he gave up his life to spiritualism, abandoned any writing that had nothing to do with that faith and devoted himself to travelling the world proselytizing. Being a conscientious man, he estimated in 1924 that in the first five years of his ministry he had travelled more than fifty thousand miles and had addressed some three hundred thousand people, some of them far-flung enough to have been of Australian or South African nationality. He deemed this to be his duty, but, to an outsider, this could be seen as not the first time that religion had played him a nasty trick: when, in 1900, he ran for election in the city of his birth, Edinburgh, he looked almost certain to win right up until polling day, then a rash of satirical placards appeared, reminding people that Conan Doyle had been born a Catholic and had been educated by Jesuits. Both facts were undeniable, even though he had abandoned the religion of his Irish progenitors decades before. The placards had been the work of a Protestant fanatic called Prenimer with someone else's financial backing, and they were enough for Conan Doyle to lose an election which he would certainly have won otherwise. Prenimer was just one of the scoundrels whom he had to tackle during his lifetime, among them Professor Moriarty and even Sherlock Holmes himself.

Ever since his youth, and given that he was a trained boxer, he had found himself getting involved in brawls with scoundrels in the defence of various women: he beat up several soldiers in the gallery of a theatre because one of them had jostled a young woman; and as soon as he arrived in Portsmouth, where he was thinking of setting up as a doctor, he thrashed a fellow whom he saw kicking a woman. Fortunately or unfortunately for him, that same man appeared at his surgery the following day and was his first patient, although he did not, it seems, recognise the doctor as his aggressor of the previous night. Conan Doyle continued to be rather free with his hands when it came to defending women: travelling by train through South Africa with his family, one of his grown-up sons commented on the ugliness of a woman who happened to walk down the corridor. He had barely had time to finish this sentence when he received a slap and saw, very close to his, the flushed face of his old father, who said very mildly: "Just remember that no woman is ugly."

A man like Conan Doyle was bound to be something of an authoritarian, at least with his family, but during the years when his first wife Touie was ill with tuberculosis, and he was already in love with the woman, Jean Leckie, who would become his second wife, his nerves were particularly on edge, and he inspired more fear than respect among his children. They were not allowed to make the slightest noise while he was writing, for if they did, Conan Doyle, wearing an ancient, demoniacal, rust-coloured dressing gown, would come storming out of his office, and punishment would ensue. Sometimes, he did not even have to shout, he just fixed them with his petrifying gaze. On one occasion, when he was reading *The Times*, his daughter Mary started asking him innocent questions about the fertility of rabbits. Round the corner of the newspaper appeared one eye, no more, and that was enough for the question to freeze on the child's lips and for her to postpone her curiosity.

To be fair, he was much kinder to his second brood of children, those he had by Jean Leckie: he would allow them to run around while he played billiards, not even hitting them with the cue if they caused him to miss a stroke. As you can imagine, he was always very gentlemanly towards his own women: his extremely beautiful second wife became Lady Conan Doyle, and he bestowed on her all the comforts and wealth of his middle years. He clearly did everything he could to make up to her for the ten years of adoration and waiting she had had to endure before they could be married, for, however much he loved Jean, he could not bring himself to wound or leave his first wife, whose illness forced him with her into exile in Egypt and Switzerland in search of more benign climates. One gathers from various witnesses that his love for Jean Leckie was such that, in order to please her, he even learned to play the banjo (badly), but that their love remained strictly platonic as long as Touie remained alive. And precisely because it was platonic, he had no compunction about confessing his feelings for her to his own mother and family and in introducing Jean Leckie to them as if she were his fiancée, or, rather, his wife-in-waiting. The odd thing is that Conan Doyle's mother, with whom he always maintained both a strong bond and a copious correspondence, immediately gave them her blessing and welcomed her married son's fiancée as if she were her daughter-in-law. Only his brother-in-law, Hornung, the creator of Raffles the thief, once blurted out: "It seems to me that you attach too much importance to whether these relationships are Platonic or not. I can't see that it makes much difference. What *is* the difference?" Conan Doyle's response was categorical: "It's all the difference," he roared, "between innocence and guilt."

He had a great deal to do with both these things not only in literature but also in life. For many years, he used to receive letters addressed to Sherlock Holmes; admirers apart, many other people would write to him (i.e., to Holmes) asking him to take up some case or problem that was troubling them. One day, however, a letter asking for help came, addressed to Conan Doyle himself. It was from a young woman whose Danish fiancé had disappeared just before their wedding; she feared for his life, and could only explain his desertion by assuming that some terrible misfortune had befallen him. Ever the gentleman, Conan Doyle took on the case and solved it: he not only found the fugitive Dane, he showed the young woman how unworthy this foreigner was of all her efforts on his behalf. Later, he took on at least two other cases, far more dramatic and complex, driven not by his desire to track down a criminal, but to liberate and exonerate those whom he believed to be innocent men wrongly condemned. After his personal success as an investigator, offers rained down on him, including one from a Polish nobleman under suspicion who enclosed a blank cheque. Conan Doyle rejected all but the few mentioned above.

Blank cheques seem to have been common currency in Conan Doyle's life, for when he began earning large sums of money with Sherlock Holmes and became free from financial difficulties, he would often send such cheques to his younger brothers, who were not as yet free from such difficulties. He was also offered cheques of a literary origin, by publishers wanting him to revive Holmes after he had made him disappear over the Reichenbach Falls in 1893. He had been tempted by the idea of killing him off before, and it was Conan Doyle's own mother— a devoted reader of the Holmes adventures and to whom her son used to send the galley proofs in order to placate her impatience—who saved the detective's life. When Conan Doyle announced in a letter to her his intention of killing Holmes off, claiming that his existence "takes my mind from better things," she replied by return: "You won't! You can't! You mustn't!" And Conan Doyle postponed the death for another two years.

It is common knowledge that when he did give in, partly for reasons of money and partly out of indifference, he first had to write a new case for Holmes without reviving him, making it clear that the events had taken place before his death at Reichenbach, and that, later on, he would restore him to life, explaining that the detective had not, in fact, fallen into the water. He resisted for a long time though. He was unmoved when young Londoners were seen walking about with black crepe ribbons on their hats as a sign of mourning for Holmes. Indeed, he was reaffirmed in his decision by the outrageous comment made by one Lady Blank: "The death of Holmes broke my heart; I so enjoyed the books *he* wrote…" Conan Doyle suffered such confusions or malicious remarks on more than one occasion: during his campaign for election to

Parliament, people would interrupt his speeches, addressing him as Mr. Sherlock Holmes and asking him absurd questions that were criminal in nature rather than political; when, after much resistance on his part, he was knighted, he received a large number of letters congratulating him on becoming Sir Sherlock Holmes. It might be thought that what bothered him was that people should confuse the two men, but this was not the case—indeed, what bothered him most was that they did not confuse them enough, and that many people saw him more as a Dr Watson figure than as Sherlock Holmes. He was aware that, in his physical appearance, he more closely resembled Holmes's chronicler: Conan Doyle was tall and strong, with a broad face, a rather snub nose, no sideburns, small eyes, and a large moustache, the ends of which he did, for a time, wax; he was not aquiline and slender, and it was not enough that he smoked a pipe and kept magnifying glasses of various sizes on his desk: he just wasn't the type, and, in a way, people thought him incapable of the feats carried out by his creation. The reason for his antipathy towards or his dislike of the character was, in fact, the one he gave his mother or as he put it later: "I believe that if I had never touched Holmes, who has tended to obscure my higher work, my position in literature would at the present moment be a more commanding one." What really mattered to the creator of one of the greatest marvels in the history of literature were his historical novels (these are what he meant by "his higher work") over which he took great pains and researched meticulously, but which met with nothing like as much success. What wearied him about Holmes, too, was that his character admitted of "no light or shade": he saw him as a "calculating machine", to which he could add nothing for fear of weakening the "effect", and for Conan Doyle, the "effect" was everything in prose.

His favourite author was Poe and, among his contemporaries, Stevenson. Although they never met, they corresponded, and he felt Stevenson's death as that of a dear friend. He got on quite well with James and with Oscar Wilde, and was friends with Kipling. Arthur Conan Doyle was convinced of his own importance, which is an agreeable way to go through life for those who manage to believe such a thing. When the Boer War began, he urged sportsmen to go and fight, and since he was himself the complete sportsman, he immediately offered himself as a volunteer. To the amazement of his mother, he gave the following explanation: "What I feel is that I have perhaps the strongest influence over young men, especially young sporting men, of anyone in England bar Kipling. That being so, it is really important that I should give them a lead." Regrettably, he was considered too old to fight, and could only go to war in his role as doctor. He was about forty years old and was, by then, already deeply in love.

Arthur Conan Doyle died on July 7, 1930, at seventy-one, surrounded by his family, holding his wife Jean Leckie's hand and that of his son Adrian. He looked at his family, one by one, but could say nothing. Many years before, he had said that the secret of his success was that he never forced a story. It seems that on that day, he did not force a phrase either.

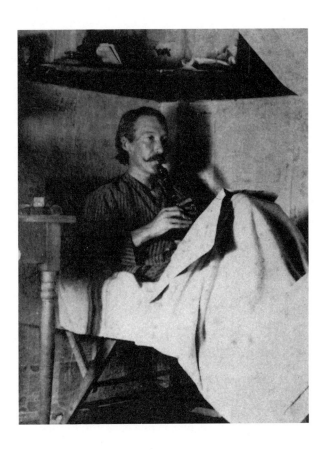

ROBERT LOUIS STEVENSON AMONG CRIMINALS

PERHAPS BECAUSE HE DIED so young or because he was ill all his life, perhaps because of those exotic journeys which, at the time, seemed nothing short of heroic, perhaps because one began reading him as a child, but whatever the reason, there is about the figure of Robert Louis Stevenson a touch of chivalry and angelic purity, which, if taken too far, can verge on the cloying.

Stevenson was undoubtedly chivalrous, but not excessively so, or rather, he was simply chivalrous enough, for every true gentleman has behaved like a scoundrel at least once in his life. Stevenson's once may have occurred near Monterey in California, when he accidentally set fire to a forest. A fire had broken out elsewhere and was spreading so rapidly that Stevenson, out of scientific curiosity, wondered if the reason for this rapid spread might be the moss that adorns and covers the Californian forests. In order to test this out, he had the brilliant idea of applying a match to a small piece of moss, but without first taking the precaution of removing the experimental piece from the tree. The tree went up like a torch, and Stevenson doubtless felt this provided a satisfactory conclusion to his experiment. His unchivalrous behaviour came afterwards, for not far off, he heard the shouts of the men fighting the original fire and realised that there was only one thing he could do, namely, flee before he was discovered. Apparently, he ran as he had never run in his entire life and as only the very wise and the very cowardly run.

He had gone to California in order to go to the aid of the American woman who would later become his wife, Fanny van de Grift Osbourne, whom he had met earlier in Europe; she was ten years older than him, married to a Mr. Osbourne (who ignored her and showed her no consideration) and was the mother of two children. She had urged him to visit her, although we do not know precisely in what terms, and Stevenson, without a word to his parents (for he was a spoiled only child), set out from Edinburgh and then, on reaching New York, crossed the whole of America, travelling in the same wretched trains as immigrants. The adventure provoked a general worsening of his always fragile health; indeed, ever since he was a child, he had endured the coughs and hemorrhages of a poorly diagnosed case of tuberculosis which kept him awake at night and more than once brought him close to death. His initial relations with Fanny van de Grift are somewhat obscure, since after that mammoth journey, Stevenson did not stay with her once he had helped her in whatever way it was that she needed help, but instead set off alone to a goat ranch, and it was not until much later, almost coolly one might say, that they married. From then on, she became not only a highly conspicuous, indeed ubiquitous wife, but also his nurse and nursemaid. Stevenson said on one occasion that had he known he would have to live like an invalid, he would never have married. He also said: "Once you are married, there is nothing left for you, not even suicide, but to be good." And on another occasion, he added: "It was not my bliss that I was interested in when I was married, it was a sort of marriage *in extremis*, and if I am where I am, it is thanks to the care of that lady who married me when I was a mere complication of a cough and bones, much fitter to be an emblem of mortality than a bridegroom." His wife, on the other hand, did not seem much bothered by that "complication"; in fact, it helped her to feel useful, and thus proud, and so to derive some benefit from the situation. The truth is that, with the exception of Henry James, who always treated her with great respect, Stevenson's other friends all heartily detested her, because Fanny, on the excuse that *everything* was bad for Louis' health, devoted herself to organizing every aspect of his life and to keeping him away from those friends whose companions—wine, tobacco, songs, and talk—she considered dangerous.

Although Stevenson was very loyal to her and stoutly defended her when she embarked on her own literary exercises and was accused of plagiarism by one of his friends, it cannot have been easy for him to accept these impositions, certainly to judge by a letter to Henry James written at the end of his life, when he was already living in the South Seas, and in which he complained about being denied wine and tobacco (faced by a life without them, he said, all one could do was "to howl, and kick, and flee"). And despite his loyalty, he did once allow himself to comment on a photograph of his wife, admitting that Fanny had left the "bonny" category and entered that of "pale, penetratin', and interestin'." To be honest, looking at that photograph and others a century on, one cannot help noticing that Fanny van de Grift seemed always to be clothed in some kind of sack-like garment and had a face whose natural expression tended to the unpleasant, authoritarian, hostile and even sour.

But perhaps harder still to give up than the tobacco and the wine were his friends, if we bear in mind that before his marriage he had led a frankly bohemian, even reprobate life. Quite apart from his various travels, most of which were undertaken vagabond-style, and apart, too, from his appearance and attire, so scruffy that, in America, passers-by fled from him, assuming he was a beggar, Stevenson also had many friendships which his strict, wealthy parents would have thought equally ill-advised. If one thinks of Long John Silver, Mr. Hyde, the Master of Ballantrae, or the body snatcher, it comes as no surprise that their creator should be possessed of an ambiguous morality, if not as regards his own actions, then at least as an observer and listener. He was always fascinated by Evil and did not shy away from certain people simply because of what they had done.

As a child, as well as harbouring strong religious feelings, feelings that drove him to hold forth, alone in his bed at night, on the Fall of Man and the Fury of Satan, he had thrown himself with great enthusiasm into committing ingenuously "sinful" acts, an enthusiasm, he confessed, that he never again felt about anything in his adult life. When he was nearing adulthood, he took to frequenting prostitutes, of whom he was very fond and whom he vigorously defended, and to participating in blasphemy contests from which he would emerge victorious, and he also engaged in a practice that he christened *Jink*, which consisted in "doing the most absurd acts for the sake of their own absurdity and the consequent laughter." But all of this was nothing compared with the misdeeds of some of his friends: for a time he kept company with a satirist who had the most vitriolic tongue ever heard in his native Edinburgh and who helped Stevenson to see the negative side of every person, every idea, every thing; this inexhaustible satirist, it seems, even condescended to God, whom he despised because of the abysmal way in which one or two of the commandments had been formulated; he could dismiss St. Paul with an epigram and bury Shakespeare with a philosophical antithesis. Far more serious, however, were the crimes of Stevenson's friend, Chantrelle, who was only happy when he was drunk. He was a Frenchman who had fled France because of a murder he had committed, then England for the same reason, and during his time in Edinburgh, at least four or five people had fallen victim to "his little supper parties and his favourite dish of toasted cheese and opium." The murderer Chantrelle was also a man with literary leanings, able to rattle off a translation of Molière extempore. According to Stevenson, he could have made a great success of that profession or of any other, honest or dishonest. It seems, however, that he always abandoned such plans and returned to "the simpler plan" of killing people. Eventually he was tried and sentenced, and apparently only then did Stevenson learn of his deeds. Presumably one has to believe him and to accept that, had he known all the facts, he would not have spent so much time with Chantrelle, but, whatever the truth, the experience appears to have left Stevenson with a certain tolerance for even the most heinous of crimes; how else can one explain his remark in a letter about Chief Ko-o-amua, with whom he got on very well during his Polynesian exile: "…a great cannibal in his day, who ate his enemies even as he walked home from killing 'em, and he is a perfect gentleman and exceedingly amiable and simple-minded; no fool, though."

The last years of his life, spent in the South Seas, provoked the irritation of Henry James, one of his best—that is, most sensible and least criminal—friends, who wrote numerous letters begging him both to come back to Europe to keep him company and to stop playing the fool. After Stevenson had reneged on his promise to return in 1890, James accused him of behaviour whose only parallel in history could be found among "the most famous coquettes and courtesans. You are indeed the male Cleopatra or the buccaneering Pompadour of the Deep, the wandering Wanton of the Pacific." The fact is that, apart from feeling in better health because of the climate, putting up with his wife, his mother, his stepchildren and the rest of the entourage with whom he always travelled, that and being given idiotic names by the natives, names like Ona, Teriitera, and Tusitala, there is little more to be said about his stay in the islands, the most anodyne part of his existence. He missed Edinburgh greatly towards the end of his life, when he knew he would never return.

Stevenson is such an elusive figure, as if his personality had never become fully defined or was as contradictory as that of those characters of his I mentioned earlier. He was very generous and, especially after the success of *Treasure Island*, he himself often went without in order to send money to his needier friends, who sometimes turned out to be not quite so needy after all, but failed to tell him so. One of his most famous proverbs was: "Greatheart was deceived. 'Very well,' said Greatheart." He had a highly developed sense of dignity, but he could also be boastful and impertinent. On one occasion, he wrote to Henry James on the subject of Kipling's emerging talent: "Kipling is by far the most promising young man who has appeared since—ahem—I appeared." And in another letter to James, written at the beginning of their friendship, he demanded that in the next edition of *Roderick Hudson*, James, who was seven years his senior, should remove from two particular pages the adjectives "immense" and "tremendous." The two men admired each other enormously, and James considered Stevenson to be one of the few people with whom he could discuss literary theory. Nowadays, almost no one takes the trouble to read Stevenson's essays, which are among the liveliest and most perceptive of the past century. When he was still living in Bournemouth, he had an armchair in which no one else ever sat because it was "Henry James's armchair," and James missed him terribly when Stevenson left for good. In 1888, James wrote to him: "You have become a beautiful myth—a kind of unnatural uncomfortable unburied *mort*."

Robert Louis Stevenson became a natural, comfortable, buried *mort* on December 3, 1894, on his island of Samoa. As evening fell, he stopped work and had a game of cards with his wife. Then he went down to the cellar to fetch a bottle of burgundy for supper. He went out onto the porch to rejoin Fanny and there, suddenly, he put both hands to his head and cried: "What's that?" Then he asked quickly: "Do I look strange?" Even as he did so, he collapsed on his knees beside Fanny, felled by a brain hemorrhage. He was carried to his bed and never regained consciousness. He was forty-four-years old.

When writing about Stevenson, one should end with "Requiem," a poem he had composed many years before and which is inscribed on his tomb high up on Mount Vaea, in Samoa, four thousand meters above sea level:

> Under the wide and starry sky,
> Dig the grave and let me lie;
> Glad did I live and gladly die,

And I laid me down with a will.
This be the verse you grave for me;
"Here he lies, where he longed to be;
Home is the sailor, home from the sea,
And the hunter home from the hill."

IVAN TURGENEV IN HIS SADNESS

THE PESSIMISM IN Ivan Turgenev's novels and short stories, with which even some of his colleagues reproached him, must have been the minimal and least harmful tribute of all those he might have paid to his terrible, not to say downright evil family environment. His famous and wealthy mother, Varvara Petrovna, was of a cruelty, meanness, and barbarity exceeded only by that of her own mother, Ivan's grandmother, about whom he told the following story. In her old age, she suffered from paralysis and spent most of her time sitting immobile in an armchair. One day, she became enraged with the young servant attending her and, in the heat of the moment, picked up a piece of wood and struck him over the head so hard that he fell unconscious to the floor. The sight proved so disagreeable to the old woman that she dragged the boy towards her, positioned his bleeding head on the armchair she was sitting in, placed a cushion over it, then sat down on top of it, thus asphyxiating him, one presumes in order not to be further troubled by that head and its unseemly gouts of blood.

There is no denying that, given such forebears, Turgenev showed great courage and merit in writing his first narrative work, *Sketches from a Hunter's Album*; indeed, legend has it that, three days after reading it, Czar Alexander ordered the emancipation of the serfs. It was also said that, on at least two occasions, the Czarina ordered the censors not to interfere with Turgenev's books, although it is hard to know whether this was a cause for praise or opprobrium. However, despite these beginnings and his many writings on the Russian question, Turgenev was, throughout his life, the frequent object of his compatriots' hatred and contempt, for they saw him as a strange, Westernized Russian, remote, atheistic, and frivolous, who spent far too much time in France, England, or Germany, mainly shooting partridges. It is true that he loved hunting, but it is no less true that he never entirely washed his hands of his homeland, and a friend's suggestion that he should buy a telescope in order to observe events in Russia was, in fact, unfair.

The truth is that, in this respect, Turgenev was a divided man, or perhaps he had to seek forgiveness for this duplicity from his close friends on both sides of the divide: in his letters to Slav friends he would revile the Western world, rejecting in particular the beliefs and conventions of the French; in letters he wrote to Flaubert, Maupassant, Merimée, or Henry James, he would complain bitterly about what Russians have always complained about, that is, all things Russian. In Paris, he could almost pass for a French author, although there was an aristocratic air about him that betrayed him as a foreigner; in that sense, it was no different when he was staying at his property in Spasskoye or in St. Petersburg, where he was viewed as a foreigner by serfs and by other writers, so much so that, on one occasion, when he arrived in Spasskoye accompanied by Ralston, his English translator, a highly significant confusion ensued. Ralston looked physically very much like Turgenev, for he too was a giant of a man, with very white hair and beard. When the serfs saw their master appear in the company of a kind of foreign double who, nonetheless, knew Russian, and who, even more alarmingly, devoted himself to visiting every house and every shack, asking detailed questions and noting down all manner of facts and words in a notebook, they thought this must portend some sinister, malign, and even supernatural purpose. They finally persuaded themselves that the mysterious visitor presaged some kind of punishment and many of them packed up all their belongings and formed a line along the road with their rickety carts, waiting for the order to leave, for they had reached the conclusion that they were being deported to England along with their master's satanic double, and that their places would be taken by a more submissive population, possibly brought, in some strange form of barter, from England itself.

Although Turgenev was a moderate and humane master, it is not so very strange, given the family tradition, that his serfs should have been capable of imagining the most bizarre reprisals. The mother, Varvara Petrovna, did not lag far behind the grandmother in cruelty: she referred to her serfs as "subjects" and treated them far worse than if they were. For example, and so as not to recount too many atrocities, she forbade her servants from having children because this would have meant they had to neglect their duties, and the few offspring who, despite everything and by some mishap chanced to arrive in this world, were immediately abandoned, with newborn babies being drowned in a pond. Varvara Petrovna did not treat her own children (Nikolai and Ivan) very much better—she continued to beat them until they were almost grown men—nor her grandchildren either, taking advantage of Turgenev's continual travelling to torment, in particular, the illegitimate daughter born to Ivan and a seamstress employed in the house, amusing herself by occasionally dressing the child up as a young lady in order to show her to her guests; when she asked who the girl looked like and the unanimous response came—her son Ivan Sergeivich—she would immediately have the girl stripped of all her finery and sent back to pine away in the kitchen, where she spent most of her time. Ivan was, nevertheless, her favourite, as shown by the fact that, after another huge argument with him, Varvara Petrovna trampled underfoot a youthful portrait of her offending son, but would not allow the maid to retrieve it from among the broken glass for a whole year.

Turgenev's relationships with women seem, then, never to have been very easy, but it would be facile to think that, hating his mother as he did, he had no option but to reproduce the same model of domination and violence. The great love of his life was the singer Pauline Viardot, also known as "La García," which was doubtless her real name, bearing in mind that she was a Spanish gipsy (or imitation thereof). She was married to a M.Viardot, twenty years her senior and whom she never left, not even during the decade she spent spurning Turgenev's advances nor when she finally accepted them. More than that, it was Turgenev who had to adapt to the situation. He apparently spent long periods living with the couple, on "fraternal" terms with M. Viardot and on more or less "conjugal" terms with "La García." She was an ugly woman with a magnetic personality, a very strong character, and considerable talent, and there exists a pen portrait of her by the poet Heine, in which his passionate admiration verges on the horrific when one considers that, unlike Heine or the painter Delacroix, Turgenev did not restrict himself to admiring her merely on stage: "There are moments during her impassioned performances," says Heine enthusiastically, "especially when she opens her vast mouth to reveal her dazzling white teeth and smiles with such cruel sweetness and delicious ferocity that one has the feeling that all the monstrous plants and animals of India and Africa are about to appear." In the end, La Viardot or La García was unfaithful to Turgenev with a painter, and their relationship was broken off, but not, by any means, for good: towards the end of his life, the novelist was writing libretti for the operettas she composed and performed, not only that, he appeared in them too, dragging himself across the stage, surrounded by odalisques and disguised as a Turkish sultan. The Empress Victoria, who attended one of these family productions, enjoyed it greatly, but expressed her doubts about whether this behaviour was "dignified" in such a great man.

Her doubts were shared by Tolstoy after seeing Turgenev dance the cancan with a twelve-year-old girl during a particularly animated birthday party. Count Tolstoy noted severely in his diary that night: "Turgenev… the cancan. Sad." Naturally there were a number of differences and a degree of friendship between the two men. These differences reached their peak when Tolstoy challenged him to a duel after a bitter argument about whether or not Russia should become westernised, and so that the whole thing would not end in a few scratches and some champagne toasts, he demanded that the weapon of choice should be a shotgun. Turgenev apologised, but when he heard that Tolstoy had subsequently been going around calling him a coward, he was the one to issue a challenge, postponing the encounter, however, until after his return from an imminent trip abroad. It was then Tolstoy's turn to apologise, and so seventeen years passed, at the end of which they stopped postponing the duel, cancelled it altogether and were, at last, reconciled. Both Tolstoy and Dostoyevsky turned to Turgenev when, while travelling in the West, they lost everything at the gambling tables (Dostoyevsky even lost his watch). Turgenev lent them money, which did not, however, prevent Dostoyevsky from launching frequent attacks on him, not to mention taking nine years to return the loan. Dostoyevsky was an epileptic and so Turgenev forgave him and treated him as if he were an invalid, that is, with a mixture of contempt and tolerance.

It is clear that Turgenev felt more at ease with his French colleagues, who venerated him. When he visited Merimée or Flaubert, they would sit up all night talking. Certain Englishmen were less warm in their welcome: Carlyle burst out laughing when Turgenev was telling him an anecdote which he judged to be extremely sad, as did that coarse man Thackeray on hearing Turgenev recite in Russian a poem by his adored Pushkin. When Maupassant went to visit him two weeks before his death, Turgenev asked him to bring a revolver with him next time: he had cancer of the spine and was in terrible pain. During his last days he was delirious, calling Pauline Viardot "Lady Macbeth" and reproaching her for having denied him the happiness of marriage. Indeed, he always referred to their relationship as his "unofficial marriage." He lapsed into a coma from which he only emerged to say to Pauline: "Come closer... closer. The time has come to say goodbye... like the Russian czars... Here is the queen of queens. What good she has done!" It is hard to know whether those last words were ironic or not. Ivan Turgenev died on September 3, 1883, at the age of sixty-four, in Bougival, near Paris. His body was taken to St.

Petersburg and buried, according to his wishes, beside his old friend Belinski, who had died many years before.

Turgenev was so trusting that he spent his whole life allowing himself to be duped, especially by his compatriots, whom he would always bail out with help and money if he found them in difficulties, even if they were complete strangers. Despite being both atheistic and frivolous, he embraced literary seriousness and a number of other virtues with far greater rigour than his contemporaries. In a little-known piece, "The Execution of Tropmann," about an execution he had witnessed in Paris in 1870, he tells how, as the moment approached for the murderer Tropmann to be guillotined, "the sense of some unknown transgression committed by me, of some secret shame, grew ever stronger inside me," and he adds that the horses pulling the covered wagon waiting to take away the corpse seemed to him, at that moment, the only innocent creatures there. This story is one of the most powerful arguments against the death penalty ever written. Or, perhaps, one of the saddest. Indeed, Pauline Viardot or "La García," who presumably knew him well, said of Ivan Turgenev: "He was the saddest of men."

Thomas Mann in his Suffering

ACCORDING TO THOMAS Mann, any novel that lacked irony was, by definition, dull, and he, of course, believed that his own novels were shot through with it, a rather extraordinary belief for anyone who has read his most famous epics. This statement may be slightly more understandable if you bear in mind that Mann made a clear distinction between humour and irony and judged that Dickens had too much of the former and not enough of the latter. Perhaps this explains why Mann only obliges one to laugh occasionally (one senses that he was smiling as he wrote it) and why Dickens makes one laugh out loud on almost every other page.

What seems certain is that the one area in which Thomas Mann never raised a laugh (not even a forced one) was in his private life, at least to judge by his letters and diaries, which are dreadfully serious. The latter, of course, were only published in 1975, twenty years after his death, and once you have read them, there seem to be only three possible reasons for the delay: to keep people waiting and to give himself airs; to prevent people from knowing too soon that he couldn't keep his eyes off young men; and so that no one would know the trouble he had with his stomach and how fundamental to him these vicissitudes (his stomach's, I mean) were.

Any writer who leaves behind him sealed envelopes not to be opened until long after his death is clearly convinced of his own immense importance, as tends to be confirmed when, after all that patient waiting, the wretched, disappointing envelopes are finally opened. In the case of Mann and his diaries, what strikes one most is that he obviously felt that absolutely everything that happened to him was worthy of being recorded, from the time he got up in the morning to what the weather was like, as well as what he was reading and, above all, what he was writing. Only very rarely, though, does he make any wise comment on these things, and so his diaries seem more like those of someone intent on helping posterity to make a detailed reconstruction of each incomparable day than those of someone intent on relating secret events or confiding private opinions. They give the impression that Mann was thinking ahead to a studious future which would exclaim after each entry: "Good heavens, so that was the day when the Great Man wrote such and such a page of *The Holy Sinner* and then, the following night, read some verses by Heine, that is *so* revealing!" It is perhaps harder to foresee the astonishing, revelatory impact of the prolonged reports on how his stomach is doing: "Not well. Abdominal pain from my large intestine," he notes one day in 1918. "Slight abdominal pains," he feels obliged to record in 1919, and the same year, he says: "Had a bowel movement after breakfast." In 1921, things have not improved, but are deemed just as worthy of note: "In the evening, palpitations and stomach cramps," or: "Indisposed, stomach upset." Later, in 1933, Mann is still obsessed, and quite right too: "Had breakfast in bed. A tendency to diarrhoea." It is hardly surprising that, a year on, he is complaining: "My stomach hurts," nor that in 1937 he is sufficiently lucid to acknowledge: "My stomach is unclean," and to add: "I had difficulty swallowing my food, which had to be passed through a sieve." In 1939, the tables have turned, and so he deems it reasonable to note: "Constipation." At least the year before, in 1938, we find a different, although no less distasteful note: "I've been without my false teeth for quite some time. Pain."

One should not think, however, that the diaries are concerned only with such banal indispositions: as well as telling us whether or not he drank a glass of punch, that his rugs have come back from the cleaner's, or that he visited the chiropodist having first been to the manicurist, there are eloquent remarks on Mann's tortured sexuality. For example: "Tenderness." Or: "Erotic night. But one may not wish for calm *quand même.*" Or even more problematically: "Yesterday, shortly before going to bed, I suffered an attack of the sexual variety, which had serious consequences for my nerves: over-excitement, fear, persistent insomnia, weakness of the stomach which manifested itself in acidity and nausea." And again: "Sexual excess, but although the nervous excitement long delayed sleep, it has proved intellectually rather more beneficial than otherwise." That word "intellectually" helps us decipher perhaps another, frankly enigmatic comment: "Sexual disturbance and disturbance in my activities when faced by the impossibility of refusing to write an obituary for Eduard Keyserling." Finally, stomach and sex are reunited in this optimistic, or, rather, credulous note: "I have had to stop drinking the strong beer they make nowadays, not just because it attacked my stomach, but also because it acted as an aphrodisiac, exciting me and giving me restless nights." The general tone is this: "Last night and this evening too: tormented by sex."

Although, as you can see, Mann was never very specific, one assumes that these attacks, excesses and disturbances must have been to do with his wife, Katia, the mother of his six children. And yet other women seem to have been entirely invisible to him, unlike boys. When he went to hear a reading by Rabindranath Tagore, his impression of him "as being a refined old English lady" was confirmed; on the other hand, it did not escape his notice that Tagore's son was "brown and muscular, a very virile type." At the same event, he was "captivated by two young men, strangers to me, handsome, possibly Jewish." A few days later, the company of "a healthy young fellow with golden hair" cast "a sweet spell" over him, and a few weeks afterwards, a young gardener, "beardless, with brown arms and open shirt, gave me quite a turn." He was enormously grateful to the German cinema of the 1930s which, unlike the American and French varieties, offered him "the pleasure of contemplating young bodies, especially those of the masculine sex, in the nude." Although he generally despised the art, so bereft of words and representative only of the ordinary man, he recognised its "sensual effects on the soul."

One has the awful feeling that Thomas Mann, far from the humour and irony attributed to him by some of his readers and acquaintances, suffered constantly from melancholy, indolence, nervous attacks, feelings of panic, and various other psychological torments, the most prominent of which was irritation. With the exception of Proust (and in an entirely different way), no one else has explored so thoroughly the relationship between illness and the artistic nature, and, in that sense, one might say he was always rather old-fashioned, since that particular link had been made at least a hundred years before he published his first novel, *Buddenbrooks*, in 1901. The odd thing is that his various ills and anxieties were very stable: they did not abandon him in any of the many places in which he was obliged to live when he went into exile from Germany before the beginning of the Second World War and after the Nobel Prize—which he received in 1929 as if it were the most natural thing in the world. What, in the end, ennobles him is his unequivocal opposition to Nazism, from start to finish, even though his own political or apolitical ideas were never very clear and did not, perhaps, have much to recommend them: he appears to have favoured, in opposition to both fascism and liberalism, an "enlightened dictatorship," an expression in which the adjective is far too vague and connotative not to be over-ruled by the noun.

The sad thing about Thomas Mann is that he really believed that he did not take himself seriously, when what leaps out at you, from novels, essays, letters, and diaries alike, is his utter belief in his own immortality. On one occasion, in order to play down the merits of his novella *Death in Venice*, which an American was praising to the skies, all he could think of to bring his admirer down to earth was this: "After all, relatively speaking, I was still a beginner. A beginner of genius but still a beginner." Once he was no longer a beginner, he considered himself capable of the greatest achievements, and, in a letter to the critic Carl Maria Weber, spoke confidently of "the great story that I have yet to write." His admiration for *Don Quixote* is well known, since he made use of his reading of the book while on board the steamship *Volendam*, which was carrying him to New York, to write a slender volume, *Voyage with Don Quixote*. However, he not only found the sober, magisterial conclusion of Cervantes' novel disappointing, he felt he could improve on it: "The close of the book is rather flat, not gripping enough; I mean to do better with Jacob." He was referring, of course, to the Jacob of his tetralogy *Joseph and His Brothers*, which, in Spain, only the patient (and resentful) Juan Benet has been capable of reading in its entirety. It is surprising to learn that Mann believed that great books were the result of modest intentions, that ambition should not come first and should not precede the work, that it should be bound up with the work and not with the ego of its creator. "There is nothing falser than ambition in the abstract, than ambition itself, independent of the work, the pallid ambition of the ego. Anyone who harbours such feelings is behaving like a sick eagle," he wrote. Given his own ambitions, both expressed and unexpressed, one would have to conclude that the illness from which the eagle Mann was suffering was nothing less than blindness. Speaking to an old school friend about death, he commented: "As immortalized by me in *The Magic Mountain*." Only someone with ambitions and who took himself very seriously indeed could gravely note down in his diary one day in 1935: "Letter in French from a young writer from Santiago de Chile, informing me of my influence on new Chilean literature." I cannot help underlining four words: the first two are "informing me," the second is "influence," the third is "Chilean."

According to those who knew him, Thomas Mann had a solemn bearing, especially from behind. From the front, his nose, eyebrows, and ears (all of which were pointed) gave him a rather impish appearance, which was somewhat at odds perhaps with solemnity. He was passionate in his public speeches, so much so that, on one occasion, he went over his allotted time during a radio broadcast and had to stop in mid-sentence and apologise. His upper-middle-class background revealed itself at times in his quarrels with servants: "Attack of rage with the maid Josefa"; "Disloyal cook, deaf maid"; "The new maids do not seem entirely useless"; and "All the servants are again threatening to leave. The vile rabble fill me with nausea and loathing," are just a few of the angry comments he vouchsafed to his secret diaries.

His two sisters committed suicide, as did his son Klaus, a novelist more modest and forgotten than his father. He did, therefore, suffer greatly, although when his sister Carla died, the pain of loss was mingled with disapproval that she should have taken her life in her mother's house and not in some more suitable place. He also suffered exile and the vicious hatred of his compatriots, he became both a Czech and an American citizen, but had the satisfaction of enjoying the most absolute literary success throughout his life, which may have been some compensation. He died on August 12, 1955 in Zurich, at the age of eighty, from a thrombosis. There were no ironic comments at his death. His family was thoughtful enough to bury with him a ring of which he had always been very proud and which he always wore. The stone was green, but it was not an emerald.

NABOKOV IN RAPTURES

VLADIMIR NABOKOV probably harboured no more obsessions or antipathies than any of his writer colleagues; it may just seem that way because he was prepared to recognise, proclaim and continually foment them. This brought him something of a reputation as a misanthrope, as was bound to happen in a country as convinced of its own rectitude and tolerance as the one he adopted during the crucial years of his literary life:

in the United States, especially in New England, it is not the done thing for foreigners to hold forceful opinions, still less to express them freely. "That disagreeable old man," is a remark that recurs among those who knew Nabokov superficially.

Nabokov spent a number of years in that part of America, always as a teacher of literature. He taught first at Wellesley College, one of the few exclusively female universities still remaining in the world, an admirable relic. It is an idyllic place, dominated by the lovely Lake Waban and the perennial autumn of its vast, changing trees and their population of squirrels. Although there are a few male teachers, on campus you see only women, most of them very young (as graduates, they're even called "alumnae"), the daughters of ambitious, wealthy, conservative families (the students are also called "princesses"). There, the vain illusion persists that Nabokov must have found *some* inspiration among those quasi-adolescent multitudes in skirts (although shorts were already quite common by then too) for his most famous creation, *Lolita*; but as he himself explained on numerous occasions, the germ of that masterpiece lay in a story from his European days, *The Enchanter*, written in Russian. His longest period of teaching was spent at Cornell University, which is co-ed, but no wiser for that, and Nabokov apparently never had a very strong vocation for teaching, that is, he took far too much trouble and too many pains over his lectures, which he always wrote down and then read very slowly, with the text before him on the lectern, and as if he were talking to himself. One of his many obsessions was the so-called Literature of Ideas, as well as Allegory, which is why his lectures on Joyce's *Ulysses*, Kafka's *Metamorphosis*, *Anna Karenina* or *Jekyll and Hyde* dealt mainly with the exact plan of the city of Dublin, the exact type of insect into which Gregor Samsa was transformed, the exact arrangement of a railway carriage on the night train from Moscow to St. Petersburg in 1870, and the exact appearance of the façade and interior of Dr. Jekyll's house. According to this particular teacher, the only way of getting any pleasure out of reading these novels was to have a very clear idea of such things.

Given his reputation as a misanthrope, it is odd how often the words "pleasure," "bliss," and "rapture" appear in his mouth. He admitted that he wrote for two reasons: in order to achieve pleasure, bliss and rapture and to rid himself of the book on which he was currently working. Once it was started, he said, the only way to get rid of it was to finish it. On one occasion, though, he was tempted to resort to a quicker and more irrevocable method. One day in 1950, his wife, Véra, only just managed to stop him as he was heading out into the garden to burn the first chapters of *Lolita*, beset as he was with doubts and technical difficulties. On another occasion, he blamed the saving of the manuscript on his own startled conscience, convinced, he said, that the ghost of the destroyed book would pursue him for the rest of his life. Nabokov clearly had a soft spot for the novel, for, after pouring all his energies into writing it, he still found the strength to translate it into Russian, knowing full well that it would not be read in his own country for more years than he would be alive.

One must also bear in mind that the person unable to relinquish that novel was a man accustomed to relinquishing many things: according to Nabokov, all artists live in a kind of constant state of exile, whether surreptitious or manifest, although in his case, these words can only be taken ironically. He never recovered (if I can put it like that) from the loss not so much of his country of birth as of the scenes of his childhood, and although he was sure that he would never return to Russia, he sometimes toyed with the idea of getting himself a false passport and then, disguised as an American tourist, visiting his family's old country house in Rozhestveno, now converted into a Soviet school, or their house in present-day Herzen Street in what was and is once more St. Petersburg. Deep down though, like all "manifest" exiles, he knew that he would gain nothing by going back and that it would, in fact, do him harm, since it would change his unchanging memories. Doubtless because of that loss, Nabokov never really had a house of his own, in Paris or in Berlin (the cities in which he spent his first twenty years outside of Russia), or in America either, nor, at the end, in Switzerland. He lived in this last country in the Hotel Palace in Montreux, overlooking Lake Geneva, in a series of communicating rooms, which, according to various visitors, looked as temporary as if he had just arrived. One of those visitors, his fellow writer and lepidopterist Frederic Prokosch, had a long conversation with him about butterflies, their great shared passion, and although, during the conversation, the aforementioned words—pleasure, bliss, and rapture—appeared more than once, the voice of his host Nabokov sounded to him "very weary, disenchanted, and melancholy." In the gloom of the living room, he saw him smile several times, "perhaps with amusement or maybe in pain."

All these perceptions must have been very subtle, since Nabokov never openly complained about his condition. Indeed, during his American years and afterwards (for he kept that nationality), he never ceased proclaiming how happy he was in the United States and how much he approved of everything in his new country. Such insistence was suspicious: on one occasion, he even made the highly improbable statement that he was "as American as April in Arizona," and in his rooms in the Hotel Palace, the stars and stripes were flamboyantly displayed above a mantelpiece. He was conscious, too, that exiles "end by despising the land of their exile," and he would recall how Lenin and Nietzsche, consumed by a sense of invincible nostalgia for the places of their childhood, both loathed the same country, Switzerland, that had now taken him in too.

Nevertheless—as he recounted in his extraordinary autobiography, *Speak, Memory*—when he left Russia at the age of twenty, the most painful thing was the knowledge that for weeks, possibly months, letters from his girlfriend Tamara would continue to arrive at his abandoned address in southern Crimea, where he had settled briefly before his final departure and after fleeing St. Petersburg. Letters never read or answered, and that would remain so for all eternity: envelopes sealed for ever at the moment when the beloved's lips had touched them.

Before Paris and Berlin, which were packed with Russian emigrés during the 1920s and 1930s, Nabokov and his brother Sergei spent three years at Cambridge University, from which they both graduated. Nabokov's memories of that place are not exactly flattering, since what predominates is the contrast between the Russian abundance he had left behind and the deliberate meanness of things English. His fondest memories are of soccer, a sport he had always liked and which he played with considerable success not just in Russia but in Cambridge too, as goalkeeper. Apparently he saved what looked like certain goals, and was the perfect embodiment of the strange, mysterious figure of the truly legendary goalie. In his own words, he was seen as "a fabulous, exotic being in an English footballer's disguise, composing verse in a tongue nobody understood about a remote country nobody knew."

Nabokov must have been very reserved in his relationships with his family, as if, even in Russia, before the diaspora and before exile, he had been incapable of having much to do with his two brothers and his two sisters (perhaps rather more with his parents). He had barely any childhood memories of Sergei, who, only eleven months younger, was the nearest in age to him, and he recounted with excessive sobriety his brother's death in 1945 in Hamburg, in the Nazi concentration camp he had been taken to, accused of being a British spy, and where he died of starvation. He spoke with rather more feeling of his father who was murdered by two fascists as he was leaving a public lecture in Berlin, in 1922: the assassins' aim had been to kill the lecturer, but Nabokov's father stepped in, knocked one of them down and was felled by the other attacker's bullets.

Although Nabokov did not achieve world fame until he was fifty-six, with the absurdly scandalous publication of *Lolita*, he was always sure of his own talent. Excusing himself for being so tongue-tied, he had this to say: "I think like a genius, I write like a distinguished author, and I speak like a child." It bothered him enormously when people spoke of his "influences," be it Joyce, Kafka or Proust, but especially Dostoyevsky, whom he loathed, considering him "a cheap sensationalist, clumsy and vulgar." In fact, he hated nearly all writers, Mann and Faulkner, Conrad and Lorca, Lawrence and Pound, Camus and Sartre, Balzac and Forster. He could just about bear Henry James, Conan Doyle, and H.G. Wells. Of Joyce's work, he admired *Ulysses*, but described *Finnegans Wake* as "regional literature," which, generally speaking, he also abominated. He made an exception for *Petersburg* by his compatriot Biely, the first half of *A la recherche du temps perdu*, Pushkin and Shakespeare, but little else. He did not understand *Don Quixote*, and yet despite his doubts, did, in the end, find it moving. Above all, though, he hated four doctors—"Dr. Freud, Dr. Zhivago, Dr. Schweitzer, and Dr. Castro"—especially the first, one of his bêtes noires, to whom he used to refer as "the Viennese quack" and whose theories he considered medieval and on a par with astrology and palmistry. His obsessions and antipathies, however, went much further: he hated jazz, bullfighting, primitive masks, canned music, swimming pools, trucks, transistor radios, bidets, insecticides, yachts, the circus, hooligans, nightclubs, and the roar of motorbikes, to name but a few.

He was undeniably immodest, but his arrogance seemed so genuine that it was occasionally justified and always mocking. He prided himself on being able to trace his family back to the fourteenth century, to Nabok Murza, the Russianized Tartar prince and supposed descendant of Genghis Khan. He was even prouder of his obscure literary antecedents, not so much the real (his father wrote several books) as the legendary: for example, one of his forebears had had some kind of relationship with Kleist, another with Dante, another with Pushkin, and yet another with Boccaccio. These four relationships seem altogether too much of a coincidence.

He suffered from insomnia even as a child, he was a womanizer in his youth and extremely faithful in his mature years (almost all his books are dedicated to his wife, Véra), but one should perhaps see him overall as a loner. The greatest pleasure, the greatest bliss, the greatest moments of rapture were all experienced alone: hunting butterflies, concocting chess problems, translating Pushkin, writing his books. He died on July 2, 1977 in Montreux, at the age of seventy-eight, and I learned about his death in Calle Sierpes in Seville, when I opened the newspaper as I was having breakfast in the Laredo.

He got annoyed with people who praised art that was "sincere and simple," or who believed that the quality of art depended on its simplicity and sincerity. For him, everything was artifice, including the most authentic and deeply felt emotions, to which he himself was not immune. He put it another way too: "In high art and pure science, detail is everything." He never went back to Russia nor did he ever hear from Tamara. Or perhaps he did so only in the long letters he wrote to his past while ridding himself of each of his moving and artificial books.

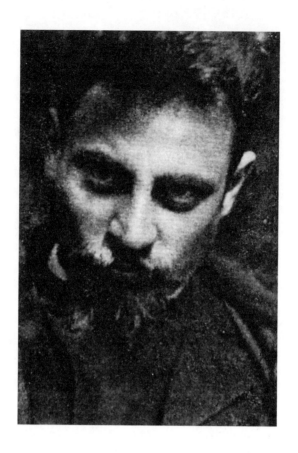

RAINER MARIA RILKE IN WAITING

WHEN RAINER MARIA RILKE was very young, he went
to visit Tolstoy, by then an old man, on his estate in Yasnaya
Polyana. They went for a walk in the country with the ubiquitous Lou Andreas-Salomé, and Tolstoy asked Rilke: "What are
you devoting your time to at the moment?" The poet replied
shyly and naturally: "To the lyric." Apparently, he received in
response not just a string of insults, but an out-and-out diatribe

against all forms of the lyric, as something to which no one could possibly devote their time.

It is clear that, in Rilke's case, the words of the old Russian master must have gone in one ear and out the other, since few poets in the history of poetry have devoted themselves, devoted being the word, so obsessively and exclusively, not just to the lyric, but to the lyric in all its forms. Rilke wrote lyrical poetry, but also lyrical prose, in his diaries, letters, articles, travel journals, and in his plays. Whenever he picked up a pen, even if only to ask a favour, he wrote lyrics, and not always of the loftiest kind. To be honest, at least in his early days, he was rather given to flattery, and he did not restrict himself merely to taking an inordinate interest in the work of others and to praising it, but on two occasions he even offered to write a book about the works he had praised: an offer he fulfilled in the case of the sculptor Rodin, for whom he worked for a while as secretary and—perhaps fortunately for him—one he did not fulfill in the case of the Spanish painter Zuloaga, although he was quite clear in his mind what the project would be like: "An ardent book full of flowers and dances." Who knows, maybe Rilke's enthusiasm waned in part after a Spanish party he went to at Zuloaga's house in Paris, on the occasion of the christening of the latter's son in 1906, and of which the reporter from a Madrid newspaper left this description: "The guitarist Llovet astonished us all with his brilliant playing, and the guitarist Palmero, in true flamenco style, accompanied the lithesome and enlivening *bailaora* Carmela in tangos such as the *morrongo*, to the amazement of the good *abbé* Brebain, who was among those watching." We do not know Rilke's reaction, but after the party, he did at least create a lyric, that is, he wrote a poem with the predictable title "The Spanish Dancer."

As we now know, thanks to the work of the celebrated

scholar Ferreiro Alemparte, Rilke's Spanish connection was a long and fruitful one, ending in a stay of four months, mainly in Toledo and Ronda, with brief sorties to Córdoba, Seville, and Madrid. He found the last two cities most disagreeable: of the Andalusian capital he wrote: "apart from the sun, I expected nothing, and it gave me nothing, so we have no reason to complain." However, he did complain about the cathedral, "unfriendly, not to say hostile," and inside it, "a vile organ, with a horribly sentimental tone." He was even harder on Spain's capital, which displeased him "almost as much as Trieste" when he left, and, about which, when he came back, he was less enigmatic and more categorical: "… it is almost as if this sad land of Madrid could not tolerate any city, and as if it had never even really wanted to be farmed either." He spent his time in the Prado and then left at a gallop; not even the Goyas and the Velázquez and the El Grecos were enough to placate him.

For a time, he was as obsessed with El Greco as he had been for a while with Zuloaga and as he would be with the lyric all the days of his life, wherever he was. And the fact is that he was never in the same place: between 1910 and August 1914, he spent time in about fifty different places, and one can only assume that, during those years, his life was not spent in any of those places, but in shuttling between them. This wandering had started soon after leaving his native Prague for Munich, Berlin and Venice. Then came his first trip to Russia and, a year later, his second trip, as mentioned above. Paris, Venice, Viareggio, Paris, Worpswede in Scandinavia, Germany, Paris, Rome, North Africa, Spain, naturally, Duino on the Adriatic, Munich, Vienna, Zurich, Venice, Paris, Geneva—an utter chaos. It is hard to comprehend where he got the money to afford all this travelling around, still less to help with the upkeep—albeit minimally and at a distance—of his daughter, Ruth, born of his brief marriage to the sculptor Clara Westhoff:

they married in the spring of 1901 and separated in May 1902, and perhaps because of this remained on excellent terms. Apart from the child, the poet owed something else to Clara: she was the one who put him in touch with Auguste Rodin, to whom Rainer Maria Rilke in turn owed one of his very few paid jobs: it is on record that he worked for Rodin "for two hours every morning."

Judging by his letters and diaries, Rilke spent his life "waiting" for the lyric and sharing that waiting with various women, most of them aristocratic (at least in name and behaviour) and happy to give him shelter in their various castles and properties so that he could wait more comfortably. He nursed amorous or merely friendly passions for the seductive Lou Andreas-Salomé, the desperate Eleonora Duse, Princess Marie von Thurn und Taxis, Baladine Klossowska, Baroness Sidonie Nádherny de Borutin, Mathilde Vollmöller-Purrmann, Contessina Pia Valmarana, the pianist Magda von Hattingberg, the Swedish writer Ellen Key, Countess Manon zu Solms-Laubach, Eva Cassirer-Solmitz, Baroness Alice Fähndrich von Nordeck zur Rabenau, Katharina von Düring Kippenberg, Elisabeth Gundolf-Salomon, Nanny Wunderly-Volkart, Countess Margot Sizzo-Noris Crouy, a certain Mimi in Venice, and, naturally, the Countess and Poetess de Noailles, daughter of Prince Bassaraba de Brancovan, and not forgetting, of course, the Princess Cantacuzène. This list appears or deserves to be false, but it is not, although, as regards at least two of these ladies, Rilke met with relative failure: the Countess de Noailles thought him ugly, and the first thing she said to him, as soon as they had been introduced, were these weighty words: "Monsieur Rilke," she said, "what do you think about love… what do you think about death?" As for the diva Duse, to whom Rilke was devoted, even though he met her when she was old and mad and already in poor health, his intimacy with her was cut short by a peacock which, in the middle of an idyllic picnic on one of Venice's islands, walked stealthily over to where they were taking tea and unleashed its awful, hoarse shriek right in the ear of the actress, who fled not only the picnic, but Venice itself. In some whimsical way Rilke identified with the peacock, a fact that brought with it strange feelings of remorse and kept him awake all night.

Rilke's rapport with animals will be familiar to anyone who has read his extraordinary Eighth Duino Elegy. Dogs seem to have brought out the best in the poet. One need only read what he has to say about a small, ugly, pregnant bitch he encountered in Córdoba and with whom he shared a sugar lump and of whom he writes: "it was, in a way, like a celebration of mass." She had looked straight into his eyes and, according to Rilke, "in her eyes was reflected all the truth that goes beyond the individual and towards I know not where, towards the future, or towards the incomprehensible." On the other hand, he felt uncomfortable with children, although they adored him. As for other writers, his extravagant dealings with the ladies doubtless left him little time to speak to them, although he was on superficial terms with a few and, during a stay in Venice, shared a valet, aptly named Dante, with Gabriele d'Annunzio. He did not, however, meet the poet of voluptuousness himself.

Rainer Maria Rilke, who, before, had called himself plain René Rilke and whom his friend, Princess Marie von Thurn und Taxis, would call Doctor Seraphic, was, all his life, while he waited for the lyric, a victim of both physical and psychological ills. His close friends barely recall having seen him when he wasn't suffering or in torment, and he himself was quite frank about mentioning these sufferings in his lengthy letters and diaries: his "constant misfortunes" kept him from "working seriously" even though he was always ready to sacrifice his life for his work (his lyrical work, of course). One example: when he was staying at the sumptuous castle Berg am Irchel, in the canton of Zurich, the distant noise of an electric sawmill on the other side of the park made it hard for him to concentrate and to create his poetry. As far as we know, the writing of the Duino Elegies took him ten years, most of which were spent waiting. When he was lucky, he would hear voices, like that day in January when, amidst the din of a storm, he heard a voice calling him, a voice very close, saying in his ear these now famous words: "Who, if I cried out, would hear me among the ranks of angels?" He sat, motionless, listening to the voice of God. Then he took out the little lyric notebook he always carried with him and wrote down first those lines and then others that formed themselves apparently involuntarily. By evening, the First Elegy was finished, but, shortly afterwards, God fell silent, apart from a few, profitable, talkative intervals, and Rilke suffered cruelly in that ten-year silence, waiting. One should perhaps ask oneself, though, just how much truth there is in the poet Rilke's legendary waiting that kept all his aristocrat female friends on tenterhooks, for André Gide—who, although he did not know him well, knew him in his less feminized days—remembered him saying that most of his poetry emerged suddenly and all at once and required only minimal rewriting. He had shown him the lyric notebook, with a number of poems "improvised on a bench in the Jardin du Luxembourg" with barely a word crossed out.

Like any good poet, Rilke did a lot of communing, not just with animals, but with the stars too, with the earth, trees, gods, monuments, paintings, heroes, minerals, the dead (especially with women who had died young and in love), and rather less with his living fellow men. The fact that such a sensitive person, so much given to communing, should have turned out to be the greatest poet of the twentieth century (of this there is little doubt) has had disastrous consequences for most of the lyrical poets who have come after, those who continue communing indiscriminately with whatever comes their way, with, however, far less remarkable results and, it has to be said, to the serious detriment of their personalities.

Rilke was short and sickly-looking, rather ugly at first glance (but less so afterwards), with a long, pointed head, a large nose, very sinuous lips that accentuated his rather weak chin and the deep cleft in it, and huge, beautiful eyes, the eyes of a woman with just a hint of childish mischief in them, according to the description of Princess Taxis. His company was clearly very pleasant, at least to the particular class of lady who most benefited from it. He had many financial difficulties, which did not prevent him from being selective and even critical when it came to food: he followed a vegetarian diet and loathed fish, which he never ate. It is not known what he liked, as regards food or other things, apart from the letter "y"—which he wrote whenever he could—as well, of course, as travelling and women. He confessed that he could only talk to women, that he could only understand women and was only at ease with them. Only for a short time though. "What do you expect?" his friend Kassner said once, when trying to explain Rilke to Princess Taxis after he had run away yet again, "all these women bore him in the end."

Rainer Maria Rilke died of leukemia after much pain and suffering, in a hospital in Valmont, in Switzerland, on December 29, 1926, at the age of fifty-one. Four days later, he was buried in Raron, beneath the epitaph which he had previously composed and chosen: "Rose, oh pure contradiction, joy/ of being No-one's sleep under so many/lids." Even the gravestone was lyrical, perhaps those were precisely the three lines he had spent so long waiting for.

MALCOLM LOWRY BESET BY CALAMITY

WHEN MALCOLM LOWRY got into trouble in 1946 during
his second stay in Mexico and, in an attempt not to be expelled
from the country, asked the sub-chief of the Immigration
department in Acapulco what there was against him from his
previous visit in 1938, the government employee took out a file,
tapped it with one finger and said: "Drunk, Drunk, Drunk. Here
is your life." These words are as brutal as they are exact, and
perhaps, on more compassionate lips, the right word would

have been "calamitous," because Lowry does seem to have been the most calamitous writer in the whole history of literature, which is no mean feat, given the intense competition in the field.

Most of the surviving photos of Lowry show him in swim trunks or shorts, but always bare-chested—with a torso like a spindle, not fat but slightly convex. This mode of dress can partly be explained by his numerous visits to places in the tropics or beside the sea and by his great love of swimming. But it would also be true to say that he clearly did not particularly care about clothes: not long after getting married for the second time, he lost a large amount of money after betting badly on the horses and, overcome by remorse, he gave his wife, Margerie Bonner, the slip as they were walking down the street. Margerie spent hours traipsing round Vancouver looking for him and finally tracked him down in a whorehouse, where she found him lying on a filthy bed in his underpants. However, the reason behind his unclothed state was not what one might at first assume, given the nature of the place. Lowry had, in fact, sold his clothes in order to buy a bottle of gin which he had almost emptied by the time Margerie found him. On other more dramatic occasions, he lost *all* his clothes; for example, in the various fires that destroyed the cabins and houses in which he lived. By some miracle, Margerie saved the original typescript of *Under the Volcano* from one of those fires. Although it must be said that if it had burned, that would not perhaps have been so very grave, given that Lowry was accustomed to losing originals or having them go astray, and, to rewriting his books again and again. There are endless drafts of that particular novel, as much because of his publishers, who kept rejecting it or demanding yet another rewrite, as because of his own dissatisfaction with it. He spent ten or eleven years on that text, which finally saw the light of day (with considerable success) when Lowry refused to make some last-minute changes urged on him by his publishers. Had he not refused, the novel for which he is famous might well have been published posthumously, like almost all his slender oeuvre.

Lowry's rapid descent into alcoholism started when he was extremely young, after a few months spent on board the *Pyrrhus*, on which he had embarked because he wanted "to see the world" (from which, it must be said, he returned feeling very disappointed), and ended with him ingesting some shaving lotion that belonged to a friend and drinking his own pee while he was a patient in a sadistic hospital. Long before his trip on the *Pyrrhus*, however, he had already encountered hell during his English childhood, at least so he liked to recount, for several of his nannies had either devoted themselves to torturing him or had tried to murder him. One of them, for example, had taken him and his brother Russell to a lonely heath, where, beneath his brother's astonished gaze, she had whipped Lowry on his genitals; another had attempted to drown him in a rainwater butt from which he had been saved by a kindly gardener; and a third had wheeled his pram right along the cliff-edge; it is not clear whether or not it was yet a fourth nanny (or one of the three already mentioned) who tried to smother him with a blanket. But whether there were three or four of them, this still seems rather too many nannies for each, independently, to have had it in for him.

There is no doubt that Lowry enjoyed making up stories, so much so that no one would believe certain tales that were, in fact, true. He had considerable bad luck with animals: one night, he was walking with his friend John Sommerfield through Fitzrovia, a bohemian area in 1930s London, when he saw two elephants on the corner of Fitzroy and Charlotte Street. The friends raced off to warn others, but when they came back, the elephants had vanished and no one would believe they had ever been there, despite the pile of elephantine dung still steaming on the pavement, something that Lowry saw more as a scornful gesture than as proof or even as a stroke of luck. On another occasion, when he was passing a cart, the horse pulling the cart gave what seemed to Lowry a derisive snort (even beasts and inanimate objects were conspiring against him); his response was to punch the horse so hard below the ear that the horse quivered and sank to its knees: although the horse suffered no serious consequences, Lowry's remorse lasted for weeks. Even sadder was what happened to a poor little rabbit that he was absentmindedly stroking on his lap while talking one night to the pet's owner and the owner's mother: the rabbit suddenly went stiff; Lowry had broken its neck with his small, clumsy hands. For two days, he wandered the streets of London carrying the corpse, not knowing what to do with it and consumed by self-loathing, until, at the suggestion of a friend, the waiter in a bar agreed to provide what promised to be a funeral as ordained by the God of all animals.

Despite these disasters, Lowry had many friends, who all agree that, although he was absolutely impossible, he also had enormous charm and awoke in them an overwhelming desire to protect him. The facts of his life are enough to make your hair stand on end, but when talking about these, it is as well to remember what he himself sometimes said to those close to him: "Don't take me too seriously"; or indeed as his mentor Conrad Aiken remarked years after Lowry's death: "His whole life was a joke: never was there a gayer Shakespearean jester. A fact that I think we must remember, when everyone is saying What Gloom, What Despair, What Riddles! Nonsense. He was the merriest of men."

Although he played the ukulele, which he almost always had with him, and although, when particularly appalled by something, he used to amuse everyone by pretending to shoot himself in the mouth or hang himself with a rope, it must be said that the facts do a pretty good job of disguising his merry nature, given that apart from the continual drinking, the fires, the visits to psychiatric hospitals, the brief spells in prison, and the more or less genuine suicide attempts, we know that in the last years of his life he also tried on two occasions to strangle his wife, Margerie, who, despite everything, never left him. On one occasion, almost by way of an experiment, he slashed his wrists, and another time, in Acapulco, he swam far enough out into the Pacific not to be able to swim back to shore. His wrists healed and the waves failed to collaborate, just as fate decreed that his hands should not close too quickly around Margerie's throat and that he and she were not in too isolated a place, where her screams might not have been heard.

He would have had more reasons of a classical nature to murder his first wife, Jan Gabrial, who, only a month after their wedding, started openly going with other men. His friends describe a pathetic scene in which Lowry was seeing her off on the Mexican bus in which she was about to spend a jolly week with some engineers and how he gave her some silver earrings for her birthday, which was two days later and which they would clearly not be spending together. Apparently, Jan looked at the earrings in some embarrassment, and then, almost angrily, stuffed them in her bag. Both his first and second wives seem to have complained of his poor or, rather, non-existent sexual performance, which might explain his interest in the bottle and his lack of interest in the whores that time he sold his clothes.

He had met Jan Gabrial in Spain, where he spent some time accompanying the poet Aiken, to whom Lowry's wealthy father paid a monthly sum by way of a tutor's fee. Lowry did not make a very good impression during his stay in Ronda and especially in Granada: at the time, although still very young, he was fat, drank wine all the time, and insisted on wearing huge Cordoban hats of a kind that no one has ever worn. In Granada he soon became known as "the drunken Englishman"; people poked fun and the Guardia Civil were also keeping an eye on him. Aiken's wife remembers Lowry walking around the city surrounded by a troop of children who were all laughing at him and whom he was unable to shake off. He stopped outside a record shop, listened with an idiotic smile to the flamenco music issuing forth, then proceeded on his zigzag course. The first time that he went out with Jan, Lowry tripped and the two of them went rolling down the Generalife gardens where he landed on top of her. Jan thought Lowry would seize the chance to seduce her, but instead he took the opportunity to tell her the plot of his only published novel at the time, *Ultramarine.*

Malcolm Lowry was a funny, friendly, handsome man. During his lifetime, various homosexuals tried to seduce him and, one night, he got so drunk during a visit to two such men in New York that, the following morning, he was not sure whether they had had sex with him or not, although, in this instance, his main concern was that he might have contracted some venereal disease. In his years at Cambridge, another young homosexual threatened to kill himself if Lowry continued to ignore him. Lowry went off to a pub and told some friends, who all said: "Oh, let the bastard die!" Whether because of Lowry or not, the young man took his life that night while the writer was in the pub.

Lowry suffered from numerous phobias, one of the most acute being a fear of crossing frontiers, something he had to do on innumerable occasions throughout his itinerant life. When the moment came to set off on another trip, he would spend the preceding days sweating and trembling at the prospect of having to deal with customs officers. He also suffered from persecution mania and, especially in Mexico, he was convinced that

Dark Powers were following him from cantina to cantina, among the tequila, mescal, pulque, and stout.

The success of *Under the Volcano* unsettled him, accustomed as he was to all those failures, and at the end of his life, he could no longer write, instead dictating to his wife Margerie, for to do the former he had to stand up, without moving, and this caused circulatory problems in his legs. After his many wanderings, he returned to England, to the village of Ripe, where he died on the night of June 27, 1957, a month before his forty-eighth birthday. For some time, it was thought that he had died "by misadventure," but now it seems certain that there was nothing adventurous about it, or perhaps the attempt was merely less experimental than on previous occasions. After a row with Margerie, she threw a bottle of gin on the floor, smashing it. He tried to hit her and she fled to a neighbour's house. She did not dare to go back until the following morning, when she found him lying on the floor, dead, and the supper she had prepared for him, and which he had not eaten, scattered about the room, as if he had finally decided to try a mouthful and had dropped the plate. He had taken fifty sleeping tablets that belonged to Margerie, who chose not to have inscribed on his gravestone the epitaph he himself had written: "Malcolm Lowry/Late of the Bowery/His prose was flowery/And often glowery/He lived, nightly, and drank, daily,/And died playing the ukulele."

MADAME DU DEFFAND AND THE IDIOTS

MADAME DU DEFFAND'S life was clearly far too long for someone who considered that her greatest misfortune was to have been born at all. It would be wrong, however, to conclude that she spent her nearly eighty-four years waiting for death. She set out the problem clearly on more than one occasion: "To live without loving life does not make one desire its end, and it barely diminishes one's fear of losing it." She never despaired, as did her friend and enemy Julie de Lespinasse, and she probably never suffered deep wounds of any kind. It was simply that she was bored.

While it is true that the French word *ennui* cannot be translated entirely accurately as *boredom*, it comes close enough in meaning and, of course, includes it. Madame du Deffand was bored and she fought against her boredom, which only bored her still more. Not that she gave in to it, indeed she owes her place in the history of literature to one of the weapons she used in this fierce but tedious battle: she was an indefatigable writer of letters and, it turns out, one of the finest. Her correspondence with Voltaire and with others is vast; indeed, the correspondence she maintained with the English dandy, politician and man of letters Horace Walpole comprises eight hundred and forty letters written in her hand, and these are only the ones that have come down to us. It is even more amazing when one realises that all the letters were not, in fact, written in her hand, but dictated, for Madame du Deffand was already blind by the time she knew Walpole. Thus she never saw the man who was the object of her almost only (albeit epistolary) love, a middle-aged man, twenty-one years younger than her, and she was sixty-nine when that cross-Channel exchange of letters began. It is possible that had she seen him, her enthusiasm and her eager wait for the postman would have been diminished, since, to judge by the portraits of him painted by Reynolds and others, the author of *The Castle of Otranto* had eyes like two hard-boiled eggs, and a nose that was too long and too far from his mouth, which was, in turn, somewhat twisted. What captivated people apparently, apart from his pleasant personality, was his voice, with the added attraction that he spoke French with a slight English accent, which made his frivolous spirit still more agreeable. Whatever the truth of the matter, the Marquise du Deffand, who, in both youth and maturity, had known no weak passions, only overwhelming ones, came to depend on letters and on herself for her survival, for, as everyone knows, the pleasure of receiving letters lies not so much in reading them as in the opportunity they bring to respond.

Madame du Deffand had been of a highly skeptical bent since childhood. Whilst at convent school, she preached irreligion to her classmates, and the abbess sent for the then famous and very pious Bishop Massillon to convert her. When he emerged from their conversation, this saviour of souls said only: "She's delightful." When pressed by the abbess, who wanted to know what holy books they could give the girl to read, the bishop threw in the towel: "A cheap catechism" was his glum response. At the end of her life, the Marquise tried being slightly devout, to see if this might distract her as it did other ladies of her age. Being less frivolous by nature, she did not go as far as the Maréchale de Luxembourg, who, it is said, after one glance at the Bible, exclaimed: "The tone is absolutely frightful! What a pity the Holy Spirit had such poor taste!" Nevertheless, the Marquise had her maid read St Paul's Epistles out loud to her and grew very impatient with the apostle's style, which she judged to be inconsistent. She shouted at her maid, as if the maid were to blame: "Can *you* make head or tail of it?" The manner in which she received her father confessor during her final illness was not exactly resigned either. She did, it is true, allow him into her house, but with these words: "Father, you must be very pleased with me; but I ask of you just three things: no questions, no reasons, no sermons."

During her youth, having already been married and almost immediately separated ("Feeling no love at all for one's husband is a fairly widespread misfortune"), she had taken part in a number of orgies, to which she had doubtless been introduced by her first lover, the regent Philippe d'Orléans. Thus, Madame du Deffand began her rather brief career as a libertine at the top, and, as she herself confessed, her direct and possibly exclusive relationship with the most powerful man in France lasted two whole weeks, which, in that court, was an eternity. An exaggerated and malicious description of those gatherings has this to say: "Around supper time, the Regent would closet himself with his lovers, sometimes girls from the opera or other women of that ilk, and ten or twelve close male friends, to whom he referred as his libertines... Every supper was an orgy. Unbridled licence reigned; filth and impieties were the content or condiment of every conversation, until total drunkenness left the guests unable either to speak or to listen. Those who could still walk withdrew; the others were carried out bodily."

Madame du Deffand's bad reputation pursued her for some time, but could not outrun her talent. Once past the first flush of youth, the kind of prestige she wanted was intelligence, and with the birth of her salon was born her legend: when she was very old, foreigners and young Frenchmen with a future would go to extraordinary lengths to get invited to one of her suppers, in order to be able to tell their descendants that they had met the friend of Voltaire, Montesquieu, D'Alembert, Burke, Hume and Gibbon and even of the lately deceased Fontenelle. One of those young men was Talleyrand, who, at eighteen, had a rather ingenuous view of the Marquise: "Blindness," he said, "confers on the gentle placidity of her face an expression bordering on beatitude."

Her eyes did, it seems, preserve to the last their permanent beauty, but to see in that lady "unequalled kindness," "great beauty" or "beatitude" was perhaps another form of blindness, since age never changed Madame du Deffand's character, for she had always been indifferent and, on occasion, cruel. She usually had her reasons for being cruel, and her indifference was a matter of self-defence: according to those who thought they knew her well (but it would have been hard for anyone to know her very well), she was so afraid of being hurt that she always got in first and rid herself of any person likely to hurt her. Her letters reveal the restraint with which, more than once, she reacted to the news of the death of a friend. She ends a letter to Walpole by saying: "I forgot one important fact: Voltaire has died; no one knows at what hour or on what day; some say that it was yesterday, others the day before… He died of an excess of opium which he had taken to ease the pain of his strangury, and, I would add, of an excess of glory, which took its toll on his feeble mechanism." This reveals a highly suspicious excess of coldness in recounting the death of someone who had, over a lifetime, been her close friend and correspondent and who had written: "I desire resurrection only in order to be able to fall at the feet of Madame du Deffand." Of the accidental death of a servant called Colman, she remarked: "It is a loss; he had served me for twenty-one years and was useful to me in many ways, I regret his passing, but then death is such a terrible thing that it cannot but be the cause of sadness. In such a mood, I thought it best not to write to you; however, today I have changed my mind…" Her reaction to the death, at the age of forty-four, of Julie de Lespinasse, was even harsher. Her only comment was: "She should have died fifteen years before; then I would not have lost D'Alembert."

While Voltaire had been her friend and Colman her servant, Julie de Lespinasse was probably her illegitimate niece and doubtless one of the people she had most loved. She had brought her from the provinces to live with her in Paris, she had introduced her into her social circle, and, in the end, Julie, a young woman as beautiful as the Marquise had once been and as intelligent as she continued to be, had formed her own salon and "stolen" from her a few of her habitués, including the aforementioned encyclopedist D'Alembert, for whom the Marquise had done so much when he was still unknown. D'Alembert, who tended to sarcasm, loved Julie, and that, in part, explains his defection, but not his subsequent coarseness: "I know that the old whore Du Deffand has written to you," he said to Voltaire, "and she may still write to you against me and my friends, but all these old whores are good for is be laughed at and screwed." One has the impression that D'Alembert, despite their many years of friendship, had remained untouched by the wit and expository elegance of his patroness.

Madame du Deffand loathed artificiality, although if one looks at her supposed naturalness through modern eyes, one can only think that in her circle there was, at the very least, a somewhat distorted view of what was natural. Her life followed a slightly disorderly timetable: she would get up at about five o'clock in the afternoon and, at six, receive her supper guests, of whom there might be six or seven or even twenty or thirty depending on the day; supper and talk went on until two in the morning, but since she could not bear to go to bed, she was quite capable of staying up until seven playing at dice with Charles Fox, even though she did not enjoy the game and was, at the time, seventy-three years of age. If no one else could keep her company, she would wake the coachman and have him take her for a ride along the empty boulevards. Her aversion to going to bed was due in large part to the terrible insomnia from which she had always suffered: sometimes, she would await the early morning arrival of someone who could read to her, and then, after listening to a few passages from a book, she could at last fall asleep. She always liked to be liked, but this did not mean that she could remain silent in the presence of fools: on one famous occasion, a cardinal was expressing his amazement that, following his martyrdom, St. Dionysius the Areopagite had managed to walk with his head underneath his arm all the way from Montmartre to the church that bears his name, a distance of nine kilometres that left him, the cardinal, speechless. "But, sir," broke in Madame du Deffand, "the distance does not matter, it is only the first step that is difficult." Of the ambassador from Naples she wrote: "I miss three quarters of what he says, but since he says a great deal, the loss is bearable." The problem was that almost everyone seemed idiotic to her, including herself: "Yesterday, I had twelve people to supper and could only marvel at the different sorts and varieties of imbecility: we were all perfectly imbecilic, but each in our own way." She could also be almost philanthropic: "I find everyone loathsome." Or even optimistic and trusting: "One is surrounded by weapons and by enemies, and the people we call our friends are merely the ones we know would not themselves murder us, but would merely let the murderers have their way." Or rather more general: "All conditions and all species seem to me equally wretched, from the angel to the oyster; what is really tiresome is to have been born at all…" Or rather more personal: "I am never contented with myself… I heartily detest myself."

Her literary tastes were equally impatient: she adored Montaigne and Racine, and tolerated Corneille; she detested *Don Quixote* and could not read a history of Malta recommended to her by Walpole because it mentioned the Crusades, a subject that enraged her; she liked Fielding and Richardson, was passionate about *Othello* and *Macbeth*, but *Coriolanus* seemed to her "lacking in common sense," *Julius Caesar* to be in bad taste, and *King Lear* an infernal horror that blackened the soul. Nor could she abide the young.

She continued dining in society until the end of her life, which eventually arrived on September 23, 1780, two days before her birthday. And thus, despite everything, she lived as she had wanted to live: the central moment of the day, she had said, was supper: "one of man's four aims; I have forgotten what the other three are."

In her last letter to Walpole, she had taken her leave of him: "Enjoy yourself, my friend, as much as you can; do not afflict yourself in any way over my state of health; we were, for all practical purposes, lost to each other and will now never see each other again; you will regret my passing because it pleases and contents one to know that one is loved." One has the impression that nothing, not even her own death, would have surprised Madame du Deffand. Perhaps she was not joking when she wrote to Voltaire: "Send me, sir, a few trifles to read, but nothing about the prophets: everything they predicted I assume to have happened already."

Rudyard Kipling Without Jokes

DESPITE BEING A VERY widely travelled man, Rudyard Kipling strikes one as more of a recluse or a hermit. He was born in India, worked as a journalist, found fame when still young, visited Japan, Canada, the United States, Brazil, Ceylon, South Africa (to mention only the most far-flung places) and yet the impression one has of his personality is that of a reserved and unsociable man, self-absorbed and, for no apparent reason, unhappy. He entitled one of his poems "Hymn to

Physical Pain," and his praise was based on pain's ability to erase and nullify remorse, sorrow and other miseries of the spirit. The man seemed to know what he was talking about, from which one must deduce that he was desperate. Another of his poems, entitled "The Beginnings," can be read as an apology for hatred, and although the circumstances of the Great War may help to explain the following lines, they still send a shudder down the spine: "It was not preached to the crowd,/It was not taught by the State./No man spoke it out aloud/When the English began to hate." Kipling himself recognised on one occasion that he was perfectly capable of a personalised hatred that was slow to forget, but, fortunately, this does not mean that he put his loathings into practice, that he devoted himself to plotting his revenge: in keeping with the rest of his personality, he tended to brood on his aversions and fed them only in the silence of his heart.

The truth is that he had few friends, either among fellow writers or among non-writers. His best friend was, perhaps, Wolcott Balestier, an American who died too young to fulfil Wilde's adage: "Friendship is far more tragic than love; it lasts longer." Nevertheless, Balestier left as his legacy a book which they wrote together, *The Naulahka*, and love, in the form of his sister Caroline or Carrie, who became Mrs. Kipling. It seems that this marriage, with the delightful brother-in-law already dead, was neither much celebrated nor very happy, at least in its beginnings (the rest belongs to the mystery of recluses). Henry James, another of Kipling's few friends and twenty-two years older than him, was charged with giving away the bride at the ceremony, but his subsequent report of the event suggests that he acted rather reluctantly: "She was poor Wolcott Balestier's sister and she is a hard, devoted, capable little person whom I don't in the least understand his marrying. It's a union of which I don't forecast the future though I gave her away at the altar in a dreary little wedding with an attendance simply of four men—her mother and sister prostrate with flu." The remark by Kipling's father is even more enigmatic and troubling: "Carrie Balestier," he said, "was a good man spoiled." James was uncharitable and, having greeted Kipling initially as "a man of genius (as distinct from fine intelligence)," later felt disappointed in him and criticised him publicly and in writing. Despite this, however, James maintained a kind of friendship both with Kipling and with the hard little person, although that friendship was not without a degree of irony or a touch of cruelty: he not only made fun of the Kiplings' almost senile passion for the motorised vehicles that were, at the time, a semi-novelty, he could also scarcely be bothered to visit the couple. One day in July 1908, James was very annoyed with himself for having accepted a luncheon invitation from them. It was raining, and he did not feel like going, and he was certainly not expecting his host to send his coveted car to fetch him. But Kipling did, thus exacerbating Henry James's annoyance, for although he avoided getting wet, he was left with no excuse.

Kipling appeared to have a more genuine and less forced friendship with a third writer, Rider Haggard, the author of *King Solomon's Mines*, encouraged perhaps by the metric similarity of their extravagant names: Rudyard was the name of the lake on whose shores his parents had met, and his rather Scandinavian-sounding surname inevitably recalls the Vikings; as for Haggard, whose first name was Henry, his surnames mean, literally, "gaunt horseman." In the Kipling household, his visits were awaited with great anticipation, especially by the children, who would follow Haggard around like hounds, wanting him to tell them more South African stories (these children, it has to be said, were clearly insatiable given that, despite having a father whose favourite occupation was telling stories for children, they nevertheless demanded still more from Mr.

Haggard). Both writers discovered "by accident" (Kipling's words) that they could work comfortably in each other's company, and so, from that point on, they would visit each other, each bearing a sheaf of papers under his arm, even writing some stories in tandem. It seems positively dangerous that so many cruel, exotic stories should emerge from one room.

One of those stories "The Man Who Would be King" was apparently the favourite story of both Faulkner and Proust, which would have been enough in itself for its author to pass if not into the history of literature, at least into the history of readers and writers. Apart from that, and long before, his books of stories had been devoured first in his native India and then in the rest of the English- and non-English-speaking world. His popularity was so immense that when, in 1898, he fell ill with pneumonia shortly after arriving in New York, and people feared for his life, crowds would gather at his hotel door to hear the doctor's report, as if Kipling were a national hero. He recovered, but not so his oldest daughter, Josephine, who bade farewell to life at the age of six, a death that only touched the waiting crowds through the grief of her father. Many years later, Kipling's son John was lost at the front, having joined up at eighteen. Two years passed from the time they were informed that he had been wounded at the battle of Loos and was missing (although Kipling assumed he was dead) and receiving details of the brave circumstances in which he had died and his death being made official. His body was never found.

Rudyard Kipling was not one for jokes: he hated any intrusion into his private life, avoided having photographs taken (although quite a number have been preserved), refused to give an opinion on the work of his contemporaries (which means that we have no idea who, in literary terms, he respected and who he did not), and would never talk about things that were of no interest to him. The writer Frank Harris, of whom Kipling wrote, "I discovered [him] to be the one human being that I could on no terms get on with," is not perhaps, for that exact reason, a very reliable source, but, nevertheless, he recounted how, on one occasion, he had an argument with Kipling about the improbability, in one of the latter's stories, of an accident provoked by the sudden appearance, on the very edge of a precipice, of an Indian with a pair of oxen and a load of firewood. The apparition caused one of the characters to fall over the edge and that was how the story ended. According to Harris, "To end a psychological discussion by a brutal accident was an insult to the intelligence." "Why?" countered Kipling. "Accidents do happen in life." Harris insisted, judging that it was simply too improbable and that "in art, the improbable is worse than the impossible." Kipling's answer was very simple, but enough to put an end to any objections: "I see the Indian," he said.

Perhaps it wasn't so strange that he, and not the American Harris, should see the Indian since, as he himself confessed, the happiest years of his life had been those of his early childhood in Bombay, surrounded by native servants who granted his every whim and by a world of vibrancy and colour which he always missed in England, especially when, at the age of six, he was transferred to Southsea, near Portsmouth, for his British education. In the autobiographical text published posthumously and entitled *Something of Myself*, he gave the name "The House of Desolation" to the place where he and his sister Trix lived for several years, separated from their parents, who stayed on in India, which gives a double idea of the Dickensian childhood the young Rudyard experienced in his non-native country. He was so tormented, it seems, by the woman who ran the house and by her bully of a son that when his mother visited him and went up to his bedroom in the middle of the night to see him, the first reaction of little Ruddy (that is what his family called him) was to cover his face with his arm. One imagines, therefore, that he was accustomed to being awoken with blows.

It is not clear why Kipling's parents entrusted their children to such a harmful place, but it is worth remembering (not that this exculpates them) that, in a story, Kipling said of a child of six very similar to himself: "It never entered his head that any living human being could disobey his orders"; and one of his aunts pointed out that, as a child, he was much given to tantrums and would scream unstoppably when angry. It must be said, however, that, fortunately, almost none of that putative childhood despotism passed into his adult life, although, as mentioned before, he was never one for jokes: during one of his long stays in America, his other brother-in-law, Beatty Balestier, even more given to tantrums and doubtless to heavy drinking as well, got into an argument with him and, in the heat of the discussion, threatened to kill him. Regardless of whether the death threat was serious or not, Kipling went straight to the police and the brother-in-law ended up behind bars.

Kipling always seemed older than his years: although nowadays youthful looks tend to last far longer and are no real measure, there is a photo of him at sixteen (and still at school) which is almost frightening: he's wearing a peaked cap, metal-rimmed glasses and a sparse moustache, and resembles a man of forty-five. He has a somewhat nobler appearance in the photographs taken of him in maturity and old age, with his abundant white moustache, bald head and the same faithfully retained metal-rimmed glasses.

He was only forty-one when, in 1907, he was awarded the Nobel Prize, which he accepted despite having turned down in his own country the post of Poet Laureate, the Order of Merit and various other titles. Kipling was unfortunate, though, for during the voyage to Stockholm, the King of Sweden died, and so Kipling arrived to find a devastated country in which everyone was wearing formal dress (the official sign of mourning), which rather shook him and put a damper on the festivities.

He was not a vain or presumptuous man, he rarely went to the tailor's, although he did always change for supper, because "after all, that was what you did, and what you did was probably the most sensible thing to do." His poem "If" was so famous that it more than once got him into trouble with his favourites, children, who, when he visited schools, would often reproach him for having written it because they were so frequently obliged to copy it out as a punishment. In his own lifetime, he was accused of being an "imperialist" writer, to which he would respond by saying that he was perhaps "imperial." Some of his public statements did not help him much either, for example, when he declared that "at the end of the war, there must be no more Germans." He suffered from duodenal ulcers and, shortly after his seventieth birthday, he suffered a major haemorrhage and had to be taken to Middlesex Hospital, where he died on January 18, 1936. His ashes lie in Westminster Abbey. He was admired and read, but perhaps not very loved, although no one ever said a word against him as a person.

ARTHUR RIMBAUD AGAINST ART

HARDLY ANY PICTURES of Rimbaud remain, and those that do are ghostly images, of Rimbaud as an adult, of the man who had nothing to do with literature and lived on the Somali coast, employed in the most various and poorly paid of jobs. Perhaps that is the second reason why we still think of him almost exclusively as the terrible, rebellious adolescent of his brief years in Paris and his months in London. His abandonment of poetry at an uncertain age (let's say around twenty) has stirred the timid imagination of every precocious writer since, tempting them to do the same thing at some point, normally, *hélas,* at a rather more advanced age: by comparison, however, every other precocious writer has been a late bloomer.

The main reason why Arthur Rimbaud has passed into literature's memory as a ghastly child prodigy lies precisely in his abandonment of poetry and the mystery surrounding it. Not that this was the first radical change in his life. It is as if every few years Rimbaud grew tired of being who he was, an idea that finds poetical support in his famous words *"Je est un autre"* ("I is someone else"), which has found such success in the world of quotations. He went from being a studious child and brilliant pupil to becoming an iconoclastic lout, doubtless impossible to get on with. His hagiographers often bemoan the incomprehension with which he was greeted by the literary world of Paris (bohemian or not), but, if truth be told, it is perfectly easy to understand why the very people who might have been his colleagues and companions avoided him like the plague and yet were quite happy to read his poems a few years after they had met him, which is, of course, what posterity does (posterity always has the advantage of enjoying the work of writers without having the bother of putting up with the writers themselves). According to contemporary accounts, Rimbaud never changed his clothes and therefore smelled disgusting, left any bed he slept in full of lice, drank constantly (preferably absinthe), and rewarded his acquaintances with nothing but impertinence and insults. He deeply offended a certain Lepelletier by calling him *"un salueur de morts"* (a greeter of corpses") when he spotted him accompanying a funeral cortège. This would not have been quite so wounding were it not for the fact that Lepelletier had just lost his mother. When another man named Attal approached him and, as a friendly gesture, gave him some of his poetry to read, Rimbaud, after glancing briefly through it, responded by spitting on those beautifully metered, rhymed and handwritten poems. When another poet called Mérat, whom Rimbaud had admired from the distance of his native village, Charleville, published a sonnet sequence to celebrate all the physical beauties of woman, Rimbaud and Paul Verlaine wrote an obscene sonnet of their own, expressively entitled *"Le Sonet du Trou de Cul"* ("Sonnet on an Asshole"). One evening, at a literary supper graced by the most important writers of the day, Rimbaud insisted on punctuating every line read by the great men with the word *"Merde!"* Carjat, the photographer, finally lost patience with him, and shook him roughly and threatened to hit him, but the prodigy, despite his rather frail build, was undaunted: he unsheathed his friend Verlaine's sword-stick and nearly skewered that pioneer of a then still uncertain art.

That, of course, was not the only occasion on which Rimbaud found himself embroiled in violent incidents, although, in most instances, Verlaine was involved as well, which might lead one to think that it was his poet friend and lover, ten years his senior, who had violence in his veins. Their respective mothers each used to blame "the other one" for the irregular, dissolute life they both led, but, in the case of Verlaine, his family had rather more reason to feel bitter, since he not only had a mother, but also a wife, a child and parents-in-law. The title of provincial genius bestowed on Rimbaud by Verlaine might not have led Verlaine's family to expect a dandy, but neither could they have expected what they found: a coarse young peasant in full, ungracious adolescence, his face red from exposure to wind and sun, and wearing clothes that were already far too small for him, a mop of hair that looked as if it had never seen a comb, and, by way of a tie, what appeared to be a piece of dirty string slung round his shirt collar. He arrived with no luggage, with no toothbrush or even a change of linen. The irruption of such a person into the prim and proper world of the Mauté de Fleurville family was seen as a bad omen, an augury, which, it must be said, proved to be the case.

Not that Verlaine had brought to this marriage of convenience a tranquil, responsible life before or after: he had given himself over entirely to two vices rather frowned upon by families: drunkenness and sodomy. At that time, however, what with a wife who was herself barely out of adolescence (Mathilde was seventeen at the time) and the imminent birth of a child, Verlaine was trying to toe the line. Nothing could have been more unsuited to such an attempt than the arrival of that wild child whose declared intent was to practise the equally often quoted *"dérèglement de tous les sens"* ("disordering of all the senses"). When the baby was born, Verlaine spent the next three days behaving in what he believed to be a model fashion; this consisted in returning home for supper and spending the evening with his wife. On the fourth day, however, he came home at two in the morning, drunk and belligerent; he lay down to sleep on the new mother's bed, with his feet on the pillow, which means—because he did not remove his boots—that Mathilde had to lie staring at the mud on them for hours.

Rimbaud's relationship with Verlaine was a succession of incidents, with Mathilde in the middle or, all too often, relegated to the sidelines. Verlaine needed both of them and could not do without either of them entirely, despite his brutality (to her) and his mawkishness (with him)—an unbearable combination. One example of the former is that whenever Verlaine used to come home drunk, his fixed idea was to try and set fire to the cupboard where his father-in-law kept his ammunition for hunting and which was in the room next to Mathilde's, against the wall that touched her bed. On one occasion the threat of fire breaking out above her head was even more direct: "I'm going to burn your hair!" he told her, holding a lighted match in his hand. Apparently, he only managed to burn a few loose strands before the match went out. Another time, he held a knife to her throat, and, on another, slashed her hands and wrists. Rimbaud shared this liking for incisions, except that this time Verlaine was the victim: one night, in the Café du Rat Mort, he said: "Put your hands flat on the table; I want to try an experiment." Verlaine trustingly did as he was told. Rimbaud took out a knife and slashed at Verlaine's hands several times. Verlaine stormed out of the café, but Rimbaud followed him into the street and stabbed him again. Just as Verlaine wounded and insulted Mathilde, so Rimbaud insulted and wounded Verlaine, but none of them could ever bring themselves to leave. The violence reached its climax with Verlaine's famous three revolver shots in Brussels. Two missed, but the third caught Rimbaud in the wrist. The matter would have gone no further, but, only a few hours later, on the way to the station from which Rimbaud was intending to travel back alone to Paris, Verlaine, in the presence of his own mother, who, for some foolish reason, was accompanying them, once again flew into a rage and began brandishing the gun which, strange to relate, no one had taken from him. Afraid that this time he might not miss, Rimbaud summoned a policeman, and the result of that natural gesture of cowardice was that the Mauté de Fleurvilles' son-in-law was condemned to two years' hard labour, despite Rimbaud's belated attempt to withdraw the charge. They at least managed to get the charge reduced from "attempted murder" to "criminal assault." Nonetheless, it seems ironic that in a letter to Verlaine shortly before this episode, Rimbaud should have written: "Only with me can you be free."

Rimbaud was a highly gifted person who never made the most of his gifts, although they helped him learn various not very useful things very quickly, among them numerous languages such as German, Arabic, Hindustani, and Russian, and, later, the more useful of the indigenous languages that surrounded his adult life in exile. He also learned to play the piano in a very brief period of time, even though he first had to practise for months on an imaginary one, for when his mother refused to hire an instrument, Rimbaud cut out a keyboard on the dining-room table and practised on it for hours on end in complete silence. This story seems to be true, or at least more so than some of the others that have become incorporated into the legend: they say (but one suspects that he himself was the source) that as soon as he was born, the nurse laid him down on a cushion for a moment while she went off to fetch the swaddling clothes. When she returned, however, she found that the infant was no longer there, but was crawling toward the door to begin his life of wandering.

Since the publication of Enid Starkie's excellent biography, we now know quite a lot about his near-nomadic, post-literary life: about the coffee exporter, the foreman, the colonist, the explorer, the expeditionary, the gun-runner and possible slave-trader. Numerous letters from his Abyssinian years have survived, and they give the impression that Rimbaud had, for the second or third time, wearied of being who he was. His appearance changed, he became burlier, grew a beard and moustache, and the only thing that remained unchanged were his striking blue eyes, which, even when he was at his coarsest and most slovenly, gave him the poetical look so essential to youthful versifiers. He wanted to get rich quick, then curbed his aspirations and hoped merely to make enough money to stay where he was, that is, to live in reasonable comfort in Abyssinia. He wanted to get married and have children, but could never settle on a firm candidate. In a letter to his mother, he asked: "May I come home and get married from your house next spring?" The desire was genuine enough, but vague, for he added: "Do you think I could find someone willing to come out here with me?" Shortly before, when he was thirty-three, he had written to his family: "My hair is quite grey. It seems to me that my whole life is decaying... I'm terribly tired. I've no work and I'm terrified of losing the little money I have." He led a frugal, austere existence, and all his plans met with failure. He would scrimp and save like a peasant, then invest everything in some risky enterprise that required enormous effort, or else he would be cheated in a business deal or take pity on those about to cheat him, lose everything, and thus be back to scrimping and saving and to those slow plans of his. Nothing turned out well for him.

Meanwhile, his prestige and fame were growing in Paris, where he was becoming a legendary figure whom everyone assumed was dead. One day, his knee became very inflamed, and that was the beginning of the illness that took him to his grave, a cancer which caused him to be carried, in unspeakable agony, through the African desert and from there to a hospital in Marseilles. He had a leg amputated and could only walk on crutches, buoyed by the hope of being given an artificial limb. But the illness progressed, gradually immobilising arms and legs, "which lay motionless beside his trunk like the dead branches still hanging to a tree, itself not quite yet dead," to use his biographer Starkie's vivid simile. He drank poppy tea and regaled the neighbours with distant stories of the past. The day before he died, when he was only half-conscious, he dictated a letter for his sister Isabelle to send to a steamship company: "I am entirely paralysed and so I wish to embark early. Please let me know at what time I should be carried on board." On 10 November 1891, he died before he had even reached his thirty-seventh year. He was buried in his hated birthplace, Charleville, with no speeches. When, already very ill, he was asked by an acquaintance about his poetry and about literature; Rimbaud replied with a look of distaste: "What does all that matter now? Screw poetry." This idea was not new in him, nor was it the product of suffering. Many years before, on the draft copy of *A Season in Hell*, he had written: "Now I can say that art is nonsense." Perhaps that is the real reason why he stopped writing.

DJUNA BARNES IN SILENCE

THE VERY LONG LIFE of Djuna Barnes was not particularly productive, at least in terms of her literature, even though, apart from a period in her youth when she worked as a journalist, it was the activity to which she devoted most of her time—well, that and maintaining prolonged silences. Her silences were both written and verbal. In the Paris of the expatriates, the Paris of between the wars, that of Joyce and Pound and Hemingway and Fitzgerald and another eight hundred thousand would-be bohemians (mainly Americans), there are some who remember her as a constant silent presence at various crowded gatherings, looking around her with an air of shy superiority. Others, though, remember her as one of the most brilliant women of her day, guaranteed to enliven any evening, with a penchant for spot-on imitations of the famous, for impertinent remarks and laughter (a loud, strange, flamboyant laugh, which did not, it seems, last very long: it simply stopped short), for making elegant put-downs and getting tipsy.

Judging by photos taken at the time, she was not so much pretty as elegant, and this, along with her great height, made her an imposing figure, not in the ordinary sense of being very striking, but in the sense that she provoked respect. She had many affairs with men and women, although there were an even greater number of men and women whose approaches failed for the most varied of reasons, even merely literary ones. The then celebrated critic Edmund Wilson, whom she initially admired, invited her to supper one night in 1921, when she was twenty-nine. Afterwards, he suggested that she should come and live with him and that they should set off at once for Italy as the first and most acceptable step in an intellectual romance. Djuna Barnes may still have been considering this proposal when Wilson began discoursing with wild enthusiasm about the novelist Edith Wharton. And that was his great mistake, because Barnes could not abide Wharton. She may not have dismissed him entirely as a critic, but certainly as a potential lover.

On other occasions, things were less civilised: we know of a hotel porter in Rue Saint-Sulpice who tried to rape her in her room, and of a drunken journalist who picked a fight with her and her lover Thelma Wood in a café. Someone tried to drag him away; Djuna Barnes, however, had had enough: she followed the journalist out into the street, gave him a piece of her mind and received in return a blow on the chin that floored her.

Undaunted, she contributed in no small measure to the drunk being overpowered and soundly beaten. A few months later, the more malicious of the gossip columns reported on how, during an argument, she had saved her male companion "from the tougher waiters."

Even in her more mature years she was not free from being besieged, although, by then, her most insistent suitors were women. Two writers younger than her, the now famous Anaïs Nin and Carson McCullers, submitted her—when they were not yet famous—to a real campaign of harassment, one from a distance and one from close to. Nin did so from afar and through literature, by repeatedly including a character called "Djuna" in her work, which irritated and distressed the real Djuna, while McCullers mounted guard for a time outside her apartment. Legend has it that this then unknown young woman would spend hours moaning and sobbing at her front door, begging to be let in. Barnes, however, was unyielding and knew how to preserve her solitude. Despite Nin's clumsy tributes (she had said of Djuna: "She sees too much, she knows too much, it is intolerable"), Barnes considered her "a little girl lost and a sticky writer" and never deigned to receive her. As for Carson McCullers, whose work she could not possibly have known, she rewarded her with the most impenetrable of silences, apart from one evening when she presumably lost patience with the lonely hunter's constant ringing on the doorbell and said: "Whoever is ringing this bell, please go the hell away." The words had a temporary and, who knows, long-term effect, for poor McCullers died years later, though still somewhat prematurely, at the age of fifty.

Although Djuna Barnes's childhood and adolescence were strange and confused or confused because they were strange, and we do not know much about them, it may be that she was accustomed from a very young age to strange situations and to being besieged, especially if what people think they half-know is true, which is that at the age of seventeen or eighteen she was "given" by her father and her grandmother (as sometimes happens in the Bible with the daughters of the patriarchs) to a man of fifty-two called Percy Faulkner, the brother of her father's mistress. This man Faulkner took her to Bridgeport for a brief period, and his surname may, who knows, have had something to do with Djuna's scant admiration for the novelist William, whom she thought sentimental. It is also true that Faulkner (the novelist) did not admire her much either, at least not officially, since in two of his books he speaks rather reproachfully of her. Many critics, however, have pointed out that Faulkner's prose style owes not a little to Barnes's own.

Other contemporaries, though, praised her openly, from T.S. Eliot, who wrote the introduction to her masterpiece, *Nightwood*, and was her champion in England, to Dylan Thomas, James Joyce (who never praised anything) and Lawrence Durrell. The latter's wild enthusiasm (he went so far as to say: "One is glad to be living in the same epoch as Djuna Barnes") was not enough to save him from being accused of plagiarism by the writer, who detected in a text by Durrell a scene very like one she herself had written. It was probably true, but it was doubtless more an *hommage* than an act of plagiarism. This happened in the 1960s, and she apparently saw such thefts everywhere. Shortly before, in the 1950s, she received Malcolm Lowry in her apartment and he described the visit in a letter. Even though he himself was a complete mess, she seemed to him even more lost: he found her painting some sort of semi-female male demon on the wall; she told him off for the success of *Under the Volcano*, gave him six bottles of beer to drink one after the other, and confessed her fears about her own novel *Nightwood*, which she had published sixteen years earlier, but since when, she said, she had written nothing else. Although he had mixed feelings about the book (a technical masterpiece, but also somehow monstrous), Lowry admitted that, all in all, "her or him or It" was an admirable, if terrifying, tragic being, "possessing both integrity and honor." Lowry clearly left the apartment feeling somewhat confused, or perhaps it was the fault of those generous beers.

It is hardly surprising that Djuna Barnes should have considered her first name as so unequivocally hers when Anaïs Nin took the liberty of using it, for most of the names in her family seem to have been chosen precisely so that no one else could usurp them. Suffice it to say that among her own siblings and ancestors were the following extravagant examples, which, in many cases, do not even give a clue as to the gender of the person bearing them: Urlan, Niar, Unade, Reon, Hinda, Zadel, Gaybert, Culmer, Kilmeny, Thurn, Zendon, Saxon, Shangar, Wald, and Llewellyn. At least the last name is recognised in Wales. Perhaps it is understandable that, on reaching adulthood, some members of the Barnes family adopted banal nicknames like Bud or Charlie. It's possible that the names owe their origin to some mystery, given that there was a vague tradition of eccentric spiritualism in the family. One of Djuna's grandfathers even had acolytes, only a few, but one of whom was the great Houdini.

Djuna Barnes had no children and was married only once, to a fellow called Courtenay Lemon, a marriage that lasted about three years, but only just. Apparently he was an easygoing sort with a slight tendency to be overweight. He drank a lot of gin, was a socialist, wrote dull, cliché-ridden pamphlets and aspired to formulating "a philosophy of criticism" which he never finished. Djuna Barnes had more male lovers than female, but if she had one great love—which is doubtful—it was the sculptress Thelma Wood. They lived together in Paris for a number of years and always attracted attention when they walked along the boulevards: two foreign women, elegant, determined, disdainful, Thelma Wood with her enormous feet which no one, meeting her for the first time, ever failed to notice, especially those who danced with her and had to keep a careful eye on them. Wood was even more cutting than Barnes, and more boastful too: when the Canadian writer John Glassco brazenly admired her body while they were dancing (those giant feet) and asked her bluntly to come to bed with him, adding, "Sorry, I hope I'm not frightening you," she replied: "Frighten me? No one frightens Thelma Wood." Perhaps she was one of those strange people who talk about themselves in the third person. Thelma was a drunk and a spendthrift, and, worse still, was in the habit of losing, even before she could spend it, the money she took from Djuna, who, on many nights, had to go out into the streets looking for Thelma, feeling as jealous as she was worried, until she found her at last in some tricky situation and took her back home exhausted.

Among the men, it is worth highlighting her love affair with Putzi Hanfstaengl, a German who had studied at Harvard and who, twenty years later, became the official jester at the court of Adolf Hitler. Even though Djuna loathed him (Hitler, that is, not Putzi), they remained in touch, and Barnes thus became the first person among the allies to know about the lower abdominal shortcomings of the otherwise immeasurable Führer. A photo survives from 1928 which shows them together (Djuna and Putzi, not Adolf): he is wearing a bowtie, has a large nose and is very cross-eyed; the fact is he looks like a murderer.

Djuna Barnes's life lasted ninety years and for far too many of them she either did not want or could not have any lovers and so she had no alternative but to remain silent. Her apartment in New York was her inaccessible refuge. There she received letters and the cheques with which her friend, the multimillionairess Peggy Guggenheim, kept her provided for years, as well as the occasional call from publishers wanting to reprint her few books and with whom she invariably grew indignant. (She got indignant with Henry Miller too, whom she thought was a swine.) Sometimes she would work three or four eight-hour days just to produce two or three lines of verse, and the slightest noise would ruin her concentration for the rest of the day and plunge her into despair. According to one of her biographers, she spent more than fifteen thousand days, that is, more than forty years, in her apartment in Patchin Place. And we know that most of them, days and years, passed in total silence without her exchanging a single word with anyone. Just the noise of the typewriter and those lines still unread. In 1931, long before those forty years began, she had written: "I like my human experience served up with a little silence and restraint. Silence makes experience go further, and, when it does die, gives it that dignity common to a thing one had touched and not vanished."

No one saw very much of her during this interminable old age. She was afraid of the adolescents who hung around in the streets. She had such a horror of beards that she even phoned a future visitor and demanded that he shave his off (she had enquired about his appearance) before he came to see her. She considered age to be an exercise in interpretation, but she also thought that the old ought to be killed off. "There should be a law," she said. The law had its way in that apartment on the night of June 18, 1982, six days after its tenant had become a nonagenarian. The few people who visited her before that date spent long hours with her and always ended up with a headache. "I've been told that I give everyone I talk to a headache," she said. The response of the afflicted visitor was: "You're so intense!" And she said: "Yes, I know."

Oscar Wilde After Prison

ACCORDING TO ALL who met him, the hand that Oscar Wilde proffered by way of greeting was as soft as a cushion, or, rather, as flabby as old plasticine and somewhat greasy, and left one with a sense of having been sullied by shaking it. Others have said that his skin was grubby and bilious and that, when he spoke, he had the unfortunate habit of pinching and tugging at his rather ample double chin. Many people, whether prejudiced or not, found him, at first sight, repellent, but all agree that this feeling vanished as soon as Wilde began to speak, and was replaced by another feeling entirely, one of vague maternalism or open admiration, of unconditional sympathy. Even the Marquess of Queensberry—who would, in the end, cause Wilde to go to prison and to cease writing altogether—succumbed to his personal charm when he encountered him at the Café Royal, where Wilde was lunching with the Marquess's son, Lord Alfred Douglas, the Marquess having gone there with the intention of removing the latter from Wilde's pernicious influence. As recounted by Douglas himself—known to his friends as "Bosie"—Queensberry was in the worst possible mood when he arrived, seething with hatred and contempt for Wilde, but within ten minutes "he was eating out of his hand" and the following day he sent a note to his son "Bosie" withdrawing everything he had ever said or written about his friend: "I don't wonder you are so fond of him," he said, "he is a wonderful man."

It is true, however, that this second impression did not last very long, and before both gentlemen took each other to court—culminating in Wilde's infamous and unhappy defeat—they had at least one other, far more tense encounter. On this occasion, the Marquess, who has passed into history for setting down the rules for that "sport of gentlemen," boxing, and for having—possibly—deprived the English public of some of its favourite comedies, turned up at Wilde's house accompanied by a boxer, who was not only a professional, but a champion to boot. The Marquess himself had been a good amateur lightweight, and was still known at the time as a spirited horseman and mad-keen hunter. In opposition to this rude pair stood Wilde and his diminutive servant, a seventeen-year-old lad who looked like a miniature. There was no need, however, to come to blows. Once the "screaming scarlet Marquess," as Wilde called him, had said what he had to say regarding his mission to rescue his corrupted son, Wilde rang the bell for his tiny, childmajordomo and told him: "This is the Marquess of Queensberry, the most infamous brute in London. You are never to allow him to enter my house again," after which he opened the door and ordered the two men to leave. The Marquess obeyed, and it did not even occur to the boxer, who appears to have been both good-hearted and respectful, to intervene in a discussion between gentlemen.

Oscar Wilde was, then, a strong man, despite his apparent softness, which began, according to legend, in his most tender years, when his mother, the Irish activist and poetess Lady Wilde, disappointed at having giving birth to a second son instead of the little girl she had wanted and unable easily to resign herself to this fact, continued to dress Oscar in girlish clothes for far longer than was perhaps advisable. There is another legend about his strength and physical power according to which, when he was a student in Oxford, he received in his rooms the unwanted visit of four louts from Magdalen College who had come from a drunken party and were out to have fun at his expense. To the surprise of the more timorous members of the group, who had stayed behind at the foot of the stairs as spectators, their four burly friends, who had gone up with the intention of destroying the aesthetic garb and Chinese porcelain of that affected son of Ireland, all came tumbling back down the stairs, one after the other.

It seems that many people have lied about Wilde in their time, and one can only put this down to the many contradictions in the information that we have about him. However, maybe the following anecdote told by Ford Madox Ford does not necessarily contradict his reputation for boldness: after leaving prison, and during his final years in Paris, Wilde was frequently the butt of student jibes when he walked through Montmartre. An *apache* called Bibi La Touche, accompanied by some other thugs, used to come over to him and tell him that he had taken a fancy to Wilde's ebony walking-stick, with its ivory inlays and its handle in the shape of an elephant, and that, if Wilde did not surrender it immediately, he would be murdered on his way home. According to Ford, Wilde would then weep, the tears pouring down his great cheeks, and invariably surrender his stick. The following morning, the *apaches* would return it to his hotel, only to demand it again a few days later. Maybe all the legends are true, bearing in mind how much Wilde, the ex-convict, had changed. Perhaps he had learned to be afraid in prison, and he was, at any rate, a man prematurely aged, with only what money his most faithful friends could find for him, too lazy to work (that is, to write), exasperatingly querulous and faintly comic. During this period, he adopted the name Sebastian Melmoth, published only his famous *Ballad of Reading Gaol*, grew ever deafer, had coarse, reddened skin and walked as if his feet hurt him, leaning always on that much-stolen stick. His clothes were not as resplendent as they had been in the past, and he had succumbed at last to the obesity that had stalked him for so long; in a photo taken of him standing in front of St. Peter's in Rome, three years before his death, his whole figure is dominated and made ludicrous by a minuscule hat that cruelly emphasises his very large head, the head which, in his youth, had been crowned by long, artistic locks and capacious plumed hats.

The only thing he did not lose was his gift for conversation, and they say that he presided over gatherings and suppers with the same firm hand and rich variety of anecdote as he had during his years of greatest glory in London, the years when he was a playwright. It was not just that he came out with endless witticisms, invented improbable puns, and improvised maxims each more brilliant than the last, it seems that he was also an extraordinary teller of tales, far better than he ever was as a writer. At any social event, he was the one who talked, the only one, and yet, whenever he was alone with someone, that person always had the feeling that he had never been listened to with more attention, interest and pity, if pity was what was required. It is true that, as regards his wordplay, he was often accused of plagiarism: Pater, it was claimed, or Whistler or Shaw, had said the same thing before him. This was doubtless true in many instances (he certainly imitated Whistler, whom he at first revered and with whom he later fell out), but the fact is that his ingenious comments, whoever they may originally have belonged to, only became famous when spoken by him.

Wilde's bisexuality is a proven fact, although the scandal of his trials tends to make one think of him as the pure apostle and modern proto-martyr of homosexuality. However, not only did he marry Constance Lloyd, with whom he had two children, there has been much talk of the syphilis he caught from a female prostitute in his youth and of an early disappointment with a young Irishwoman whom he courted doggedly for two years, at the end of which time she married Bram Stoker. (One can only conclude, incidentally, that the young woman in question had a taste for strong emotions, and, having hesitated between the future authors of *The Picture of Dorian Gray* and *Dracula*, she opted, in the end, for immortal vampirism rather than a pictorial and not very enduring pact with the Devil.) And several of his friends and acquaintances were amazed when the scandal broke and they learned what the charges were: they would never have suspected him of such proclivities, they said, despite Wilde's repeated professions of Hellenism from his student days on and ever since his trip to Greece, which resulted in a photograph of the traveller in full-skirted local dress and in his formal embrace of paganism, to the detriment of the Catholicism he had been considering taking up shortly before. He had even adorned his rooms at Oxford with pictures of the Pope and of Cardinal Manning, but when he actually visited the former, at an audience in Rome arranged by his extremely Catholic and extremely wealthy friend Hunter Blair, he maintained a sullen silence throughout and thought the whole encounter dreadful; afterwards, he closeted himself in his hotel room and emerged bearing an apposite sonnet. The worst came later: as they were passing the Protestant cemetery, Wilde insisted on stopping and prostrating himself before the grave of Keats, a far humbler obeisance than he had offered to the very pious Pius IX.

Little is known of Constance Lloyd Wilde, except that she viewed her husband with a mixture of disapproval and sweetness. On the other hand, a great deal is known about Lord Alfred Douglas, or "Bosie," thanks largely to the various books he himself wrote during his long life (he died in 1945 at the age of seventy-five), divided equally between poetry and volumes of more or less autobiographical and justificatory prose. As a young man he was long on ringlets and short on intelligence, and, in later years, he lost the ringlets, but gained not a jot in intelligence: he became a Catholic and a puritan, and his judgement about what happened seems confused to say the least. It was his fate to live for far too long marked by a scandal in which he was only the reluctant co-protagonist, but he never did anything to justify his taking centre stage for any other reason. Two years after Wilde's death, he married a poetess, and so one might say that he made an odd marriage—of versifiers. His bête noire was Robert Ross, who not only manipulated and kept the long letter that Wilde had written to "Bosie" from prison and which is now known as *De Profundis*, but was the remote instigator of that whole tragedy, having initiated the youthful Wilde into sex in its most Hellenistic vein.

Wilde's witticisms are legion, and most have found too warm a reception in quotation heaven to repeat them here. Indeed, even now, he is attributed with ingenious comments that never even occurred to him. This description of a hard day in a writer's life is, however, definitely his: "This morning," he said, "I took out a comma, and this afternoon, I put it back again."

Later, he seemed to take these words literally, after leaving the prison in which he had spent two years doing hard labour. Although it was clear that if he wrote a new comedy or a novel, money would rain down on him and his poverty would be at an end, he had neither the strength nor the will to write. As he put it, he had known suffering and could not sing its praises; he hated it, but he had known it, and that is why he could not now sing the praises of what had always hitherto inspired him: pleasure and joy. "Everything that happens to me," he said, "is symbolic and irrevocable." During those years, André Gide described him as "a poisoned creature." He drank too much, which further irritated the reddened skin of his face and body: he often had to scratch himself, for which he apologised. He wrote to a friend: "I am more like a great ape than ever, I hope you will give me a lunch and not a nut."

Six years before his fall from grace, he had written this: "Life sells everything too dear, and we buy the most wretched of its secrets at a monstrous, infinite price." He stopped paying that price on November 30, 1900, when he died in Paris at the age of forty-six, after a death agony that lasted more than two months. The cause of his death was an ear infection which later spread and was vaguely syphilitic in origin. Legend has it that shortly before he died, he called for champagne and, when it was brought it to him, said cheerfully: "I am dying beyond my means." He lies in the Paris cemetery of Père Lachaise, and on his grave, presided over by a sphinx, there is never any shortage of the flowers due to all martyrs.

YUKIO MISHIMA IN DEATH

THE DEATH OF Yukio Mishima was so spectacular that it
has almost succeeded in obliterating the many other stupid
things he did in his life, as if his previous non-stop exhibition-
ism had been merely a way of getting people's attention for the
culminating moment, doubtless the only one that really interested him. That, at least, is how we must see it, as coming from
his deep-rooted fascination with violent death, which—if the
victim was young and had a good body—he considered to be

the height of beauty. It is true that this idea was not entirely original to him, still less in his country, Japan, where, as we know, there has always been a highly respected tradition of ceremonial self-disembowelment followed immediately by decapitation with a single blow delivered by a friend or subordinate. Not so very long ago, at the end of the Second World War, no fewer than five hundred officers (as well as a fair number of civilians) committed suicide as a way of "taking responsibility" for the defeat and "presenting their apologies to the Emperor." Among them was a friend of Mishima's, Zenmei Hasuda, who, before honouring "the culture of my country, which, I am sure, approves of those who die young" and blowing his brains out, still had time to murder his immediate superior for having criticised the divine Emperor. Perhaps it is understandable that twenty-five years later, the Japanese army was, as Mishima put it, still depressed, vulnerable, and incapable of hitting back.

His desire for death, born at an early age, was not, however, indiscriminate, and while one can understand his terror of being poisoned, since death by such means could hardly be called "beautiful," it is not so easy to explain why, in 1945, when he was called up at the age of twenty, he took advantage of a temporary fever brought on by a bout of flu to lie to the army doctor examining him and to present him with a list of fictitious symptoms that prompted the doctor to make an erroneous diagnosis of incipient tuberculosis and to exempt him from military service. Not that Mishima was unaware of the implications this had for the veracity of his ideals: on the contrary, in his famous autobiographical novel, *Confessions of a Mask*, he pondered this matter very pompously and at great length. As one would expect from a man of considerable cunning, he finally came up with an aesthetic justification for having avoided what he, in principle, desired so much (namely: "What I wanted was to die among strangers, untroubled, beneath a cloudless sky...") and he concluded that "I much preferred to think of myself instead as a person who had been forsaken even by Death... I delighted in picturing the curious agonies of a person who wanted to die but had been refused by Death. The degree of mental pleasure I thus obtained seemed almost immoral." Whatever the truth, the fact is that Mishima did not undergo any great or strange sufferings until the day of his real death, and that, when the time came, he had, thanks to pure ignorance, all his strength and determination intact. Prior to this, though, his fear of being poisoned was so obsessive that, whenever he went to a restaurant, he would only order dishes that did not lend themselves to poisoning and, after eating, would frantically brush his teeth with soda water.

None of this prevented him from fantasising as much as he wanted, not only about his own erotic (i.e., violent) extinction, but about that of many other fictional beings, all of them extremely good-looking: "The weapon of my imagination slaughtered many a Grecian soldier, many white slaves of Arabia, princes of savage tribes, hotel elevator boys, waiters, young toughs, army officers, circus roustabouts... I would kiss the lips of those who had fallen to the ground and were still twitching." Needless to say, he also enjoyed his share of cannibalistic daydreams, whose favourite object was a rather athletic school friend: "I thrust the fork upright into the heart. A fountain of blood struck me full in the face. Holding the knife in my right hand, I began carving the flesh of his breast, gently, thinly at first..." One assumes that in these alimentary imaginings he must, fortunately, have lost his fear of being poisoned.

This erotic fascination with manly bodies tortured, dismembered, flayed, butchered or impaled had marked Mishima since adolescence. He was immodest enough as a writer to ensure that posterity was kept au fait with his ejaculations, from which one must deduce that he lay great store by them; and so we are obliged to know that he had his first ejaculation whilst contemplating a reproduction of the torso of St Sebastian whom Guido Reni had painted pierced with arrows. It is therefore not surprising that, as an adult, he was given to having artistic-cum-muscleman photographs taken of himself, and that he appeared in one of them in the same garb, that is, with a coarse white cloth knotted loosely about his loins and with a couple of arrows stuck in his sides, his arms aloft and his wrists bound with rope. This last detail is not without importance, given that his favourite masturbatory image (which he was also kind enough to record) were armpits, very hairy and, one fears, very smelly. This famous photograph must, therefore, have served his narcissism well.

Other photographs which he bequeathed to the more infantile enthusiasts of calendar sex were no less comic: Mishima standing before a large mirror, gazing at his own rather puny chest; Mishima with a pyromaniac glint in his eye and a white rose in his mouth; Mishima doing weight-training in order to develop some decent biceps; Mishima half-naked and pulling in his stomach, with a bandanna around his head, a samurai sword in his hands, and an expression on his face that verges on the apoplectic; Mishima wearing a paramilitary uniform, which is surprisingly restrained given that he himself dreamed up the design for his own private army, the Tatenokai. He also acted in his own films or in B-movies about *yakuza* or Japanese gangsters; he recorded songs and made a record on which he played all forty characters in one of his own plays. He was so concerned about his image that he always made sure that in any photo in which he appeared alongside much taller men, he was the one who looked like a giant.

One should not infer, however, that Yukio Mishima spent his life worrying only about such folkloric nonsense. He must also have written non-stop, for at his death he left over one hundred volumes, and it is known that he wrote one of them, eighty pages long, while holed up in a hotel in Tokyo for just three days. To all this activity must be added his campaign of self-promotion, which took him on numerous trips to Europe and America and caused him to attempt a carefully planned, but ill-fated bit of stage-management when, in 1967, it was rumoured that the Nobel Prize was about to be given to a Japanese author for the first time. He organised his return from a tour to coincide with the date on which the decision would be announced, and reserved a VIP suite in a downtown hotel. However, when the plane landed and he was the first to emerge, laughing and smiling, he found the airport plunged in gloom because the prize had gone to some wretched Guatemalan. A year later, his depression only deepened: the Nobel prize did, at last, go to Japan, but to his friend and teacher Yasunari Kawabata. Mishima opted for a bit of reflected glory: he rushed to Kawabata's house so as to be the first to be seen congratulating him and at least appear in the photos. Needless to say, Mishima considered himself to be not only worthy of the Nobel Prize but—quite simply—a genius. "I want to identify my literary work with God," he said once to an extreme right-wing fanatic, who was, perhaps, accustomed to such delusions of grandeur.

According to those who knew him, Mishima was an extremely likeable man with a lively sense of humour, although his laugh was wild and strident and he was rather too prodigal with it. He had few relationships with women, apart from his grandmother (who, to the despair of her daughter-in-law, practically kidnapped him at birth), his mother, his sister, his wife, and his daughter, the essential female elements not even a misogynist can dispense with. He married because of a false alarm: his mother was believed to be dying of cancer, and Mishima thought he would make a last gift to her by marrying:

she would die more peacefully knowing that the family line would be continued. Her cancer turned out to be a mere phantom and she went on to survive her son, but by the time Mishima learned about the first of these facts, he was already married to Yoko Sugiyama, a young woman from a good family, who, one assumes, fulfilled the six prerequisites that the bridegroom had stipulated to the matchmakers: the bride should be neither a blue-stocking nor a celebrity hunter; she must wish to be married to Kimitake Hiraoka (his real name), the private citizen, not to Yukio Mishima, the writer; she should be no taller than her husband, even in high heels; she must be pretty and have a round face; she must be prepared to look after her parents-in-law and be capable of running the home efficiently; lastly, she must not disturb Mishima while he was working. The truth is that little more is known of her after the wedding, although the writer's hagiographers (among them the gushing and later gushed over Marguerite Yourcenar) described excitedly how Mishima often took Yoko with him on his trips abroad, which was not the custom among Japanese men of his day. With that, in the view of Yourcenar and others, he had apparently done his duty: after all, he could easily have left her at home.

It was in the latter period of his life that Mishima created the paramilitary organisation Tatenokai, to which he liked to refer by its English initials, the SS (Shield Society). It was a small army of a hundred men, tolerated and encouraged by the Japanese Armed Forces. The one hundred men were mostly students and staunch admirers, devoted to the Emperor and to Japan's most ancient traditions. For a time, they restricted themselves to camping expeditions, tactical exercises, pseudomilitary manoeuvres, and to cutting themselves in order to mingle and drink each other's blood. Their first and last real action took place on November 25, 1970, when Mishima and four of his acolytes presented themselves in their mustard-brown uniforms at the Ichigaya base in Toyko. They had an appointment there with General Mashita, to whom they were going to pay their respects and show a valuable antique Samurai sword, doubtless well worth seeing. Once in the general's office, the five fake soldiers tied his hands, barricaded themselves in, brandishing knives and swords, and demanded that the troops should gather underneath the balcony to listen to a speech by Mishima. Some unarmed officers (the Japanese army is not allowed to use arms against civilians) tried to overpower them and were badly cut (Mishima almost sliced off the hand of a sergeant). When he managed, at last, to address the troops, his words were not exactly well received: the soldiers kept interrupting him by hurling insults like "Kiss my ass!" or *"Bakayaro!"*, which is difficult to translate, although it seems the closest equivalent would be "Go screw your own mother!" (Some people, however, say that it means nothing more than "dimwit".)

Things did not go entirely to plan. Mishima went back into the office and prepared to commit hara-kiri. He had asked his right-hand man and possible lover, Masakatsu Morita, to curtail his suffering by decapitating him with the precious sword as soon as he, Mishima, had disembowelled himself. But Morita (who was also going to commit hara-kiri afterwards) failed no fewer than three times, cutting, instead, deep into Mishima's shoulders, back and neck, but failing to sever his head. Another of the acolytes, Furu-Koga, more skilled and less nervous, snatched the sword from him and carried out the decapitation himself. Then he did the same with Morita, who hadn't been up to the task in the first place and had only managed to make a shallow scratch across his own belly with his dagger. The two heads lay on the carpet. Mishima was forty-five and, theatrical to the last, had, it is said, delivered his latest novel to his publisher that very morning. On one occasion, he had said that hara-kiri was "the ultimate act of masturbation." His father found out what had happened from the television. When he heard the news of the attack on Ichigaya, he thought: "Oh, no, now I'm going to have to go and apologise to the police and everyone else." When he heard about the rest, the hara-kiri and the decapitation, he confessed later on: "I didn't feel particularly surprised: my brain just rejected the information."

LAURENCE STERNE AT THE END

ALTHOUGH HE CAME from a good enough family, with an archbishop among his forebears, it was Laurence Sterne's fate to be the son of one of its most unfortunate members, Roger, who, having chosen a career in the army, never rose above the rank of standard-bearer. Roger Sterne travelled ceaselessly with his battered regiment, accompanied by his wife and their variable number of children: variable because some were always being born and others were always dying; Laurence, who came into the world in Ireland, was one of the few permanent ones. His father, then, left him almost nothing but the undeniable sense of humour which he possessed and displayed to the end: during the siege of Gibraltar in 1731, he got embroiled in a duel with a comrade, provoked, apparently, by some absurd argument over a goose. The fight between Captain Philips and Roger Sterne took place in a room, and the former lunged at the latter with such force that not only did he run him through, but the tip of his sword remained stuck fast in the wall. Showing remarkable presence of mind, the poor standard-bearer asked very courteously if, before withdrawing the blade, his colleague would be so kind as to clean off any plaster that might be cling-ing to the tip, as he would find it most disagreeable to have it introduced into his system. He lived on for a few more months after this incident, long enough for him to be dispatched to Jamaica, where he died of a fever which his broken body was unable to withstand. Laurence was seventeen at the time.

With the help of some wealthier relatives, he was able to study at Cambridge and subsequently entered the church, less out of devotion than tradition and convenience, and for many years, led a modest and anonymous life as a vicar in Yorkshire. He married a rather ugly woman, Elizabeth Lumley, whom, nevertheless, it took him two years to woo. On receiving the (false) news that her son had married an heiress, his mother, who had lavished little care on him and lived, anyway, in Ireland, tried to force him to lavish some care on her, without, incidentally, much success. The truth is that her son had very slender means, which did not, however, prevent him from hav-ing fun, especially during the periods he spent at Skelton Castle (re-named Crazy Castle by its visitors), the property of his indolent and affluent friend John Hall-Stevenson. In provincial imitation of the Monks of Medmenham Abbey—a group of aristocrats in the south of England, famous at the time for their scandalous goings-on—they created the Demoniacs. This club was even more innocuous than its model, which is, perhaps, why it lasted longer, for the Medmenham "monks" disbanded shortly afterwards, when one of their members, in the middle of a black mass, had the unfortunate idea of releasing a baboon which, to the great alarm of all those present, leapt onto the shoulders of the celebrant, Lord Sandwich, and was assumed to be the Devil himself, who had, to everyone's horror, finally deigned to visit them. Sterne and Hall-Stevenson's Demoniacs, on the other hand, simply drank burgundy, made music (Sterne's preferred instrument was the violin) and danced sarabandes. The favourite pastime of the jolly vicar and his idle friend was, however, to drive in their chaises to Saltburn and run races along the five-mile stretch of beach, with one wheel in the sea.

The first piece that Sterne wrote was a sarcastic pamphlet, provoked by a terrible row over local politics involving a ridiculous midwife from York. Its unexpected success was such that only then did it occur to him that he could perhaps write something for publication, his incomparable *Tristram Shandy*. This belated beginning belies the fact that Sterne had long nurtured a passionate interest not only in literature (he adored Cervantes, Rabelais, Lucian, Montaigne, and Robert Burton, all of whom he now and then openly and blatantly plagiarised), but in all manner of eccentric books; in his library there were treatises on fortifications and on obstetrics, studious surveys of long noses as well as one of his favourite books, *Le Moyen de parvenir*, by the Canon of Tours, Béroalde de Verville.

His whole life changed with the publication and unforeseen success of the first two volumes of *Tristram Shandy*: at the age of forty-six, Sterne started leading the kind of life most guaranteed to please him, a life of fun and generous hospitality. From then on, his visits to London became more frequent, and there he formed immediate friendships with some of the most influential people of the day, notably with that prince of actors, David Garrick, and with the artist Reynolds, who took the trouble to paint his elongated figure three times, although the last of these pictures remained unfinished. Sterne was the object of enormous curiosity, everyone wanted to meet him and Sterne duly met everyone, with the astonishing result that many people spoke well of him and no one spoke ill. Sterne, it seems, was not only exceptionally amusing, capable of coming up with jokes and digressions on any given subject, regardless of whether he knew anything about it or not, he was also, by nature, a very cordial and amiable fellow. This did not, however, prevent him from getting annoyed when his barbed comments were not understood or enjoyed or from taking on pompous fools with a gentle sarcasm that only wounded when it was too late for the belatedly irate victim to react. He even dined with the Duke of York, brother of the Prince of Wales, and it was perhaps not so very odd that this Duke should seek out his pleasant company, bearing in mind that the Duke died a few years later in France from a bad cold and a fever brought on by having spent the whole night dancing. Sterne's fame reached such heights that he once received a letter addressed simply to: "Tristram Shandy, Europe."

However, not everyone liked the novel or the man, and among the most disdainful was Horace Walpole, the man so loved by Madame du Deffand. Perhaps that was why Sterne, on one of his many trips to Paris, went not to her salon, but to that of her rival, Julie de Lespinasse, and to the no less famous salon of Baron d'Holbach, where he became great friends with Diderot, whom he used to keep supplied with English books. The first time he crossed the Channel, he did so, in his own words, "in a race with Death," from which, on that first leg, he would emerge victorious: his health was never very good, and, ill with tuberculosis, he suffered frequent haemorrhages which again and again brought him very close to the edge. It may be that, like so many of his best compatriots, he was also escaping a little from England: the eminent and powerful Dr. Johnson had turned his back on him, not just because of his writings, which he despised, but because, at a gathering in Reynolds' house, Sterne had dared to display in his presence "a drawing too indecently gross to have delighted even a brothel." Given the state of Sterne's health, it is not perhaps surprising, therefore, that while he was in Paris, the rumour in London was that he had died, indeed, obituaries were published and, in the village of Coxwold, where he lived when not in the capital, his parishioners duly mourned him. A few weeks later, Sterne said only that the news was "premature." On the Continent, on the other hand, he won the admiration of Voltaire, attended performances by the Comédie Française (which bored him) and heard sermons by the King of Poland's private preacher, a priest who, it seems, outdid even Garrick in his interpretations. He also went for long walks, and his long, black-clothed body and his long nose never failed to attract attention, so much so that, on one occasion, he apparently obliged the crowd following him to kneel down with him on the Pont-Neuf before the statue of Henry IV.

He described his wanderings on the Continent in his masterpiece, *A Sentimental Journey through France and Italy*, and the Sternes took such a liking to these countries and their climates that his wife Elizabeth and their daughter Lydia settled in the south of that first-named country, thus sanctioning the unofficial separation of husband and wife. Later on, a French Marquis and aspiring son-in-law wrote to tell him briefly of his love for Lydia, going on to ask the fundamental question: "What fortune would you give your daughter at present and how much at your death?" Sterne replied: "Sir, I shall give her ten thousand pounds the day of marriage. My calculation is as follows—she is not eighteen, you are sixty-two, there goes five thousand pounds—then, Sir, you at least think her not ugly, she has many accomplishments, speaks Italian, French, plays upon the guitar, and as I fear you play upon no instrument whatever, I think you will be happy to take her on my terms, for here finishes the account of the ten thousand pounds." Sterne never panicked, and when his house in Yorkshire was burned to the ground, what most upset him was not the loss of the house, he said, "but the strange unaccountable conduct of my poor, unfortunate curate, not in *setting fire* to the house, for I do not accuse him of it, God knows, or anyone else either; but in *setting off* the moment after it happened, and flying like Paul to Tarsus, through fear of persecution from me."

Indeed, it is difficult to imagine Sterne pursuing anyone. He was a kindly, easy-going man, who once tried to "inherit" two children left behind by a poor widow on her death, and he also, at the request of a slave called Ignatius Sancho, included a few pages speaking out against slavery in the later volumes of *Tristram Shandy*. He made it fashionable in the society of his time to follow the lead of his character Uncle Toby and brush bothersome flies gently away, rather than kill them. He had several love affairs and, in a letter to Eliza, his last and most idealised lover, he showed good humour in the face of the death that was fast gaining on him: "I'm going," he wrote by way of farewell (she was with her husband in India); but as the day progressed, and finding that he did not feel quite so bad, he added: "I am a little better, so shall not depart as I apprehended." An acquaintance of his described his character thus: "… everything is rose-coloured to this happy mortal, and whatever appears to other eyes in a sad or melancholy aspect presents to his an appearance of gaiety or laughter. He pursues only pleasure and he is not like others who, when they are tearful, no longer can enjoy life, for he drinks the bowl to the last drop even though it provides not enough to quench a thirst like his."

Judging from his letters, he battled to the end in that race that had begun while crossing the Channel years before. To a woman friend he wrote: "I am ill—very ill— yet I feel my Existence Strongly, and something like revelation along with it, which tells I shall not dye—but live, & yet another man would set his house in order." Shortly before he died, he started writing a "most comic romance," and saw in this an advantage: "…when I am dead, my name will be placed in the list of those heroes who died in a jest," a list headed by Cervantes and followed by Scarron and his beloved Verville. Nothing remains of that "romance," and in London, at four in the afternoon, on March 18, 1768, at the age of fifty-four, Sterne finally lost his race.

The vicissitudes suffered by his corpse are worthy of his two novels. He was buried with little fuss at the cemetery of a church in Hanover Square, but his body was stolen from there a few days later and sold to the professor of anatomy at the University of Cambridge, the place where he himself had studied. Apparently, when the dissection of the corpse was nearing its end, one of the two friends whom the professor had invited to witness the session accidentally uncovered the face of the dead man and recognised Sterne, to whom he had been introduced not long before. The guest fainted, and the professor, when he realised the illustrious nature of the person he had submitted to the scalpel, took care, at least, to preserve the skeleton. Various people have tried and failed to identify Sterne's skull among the Cambridge collection of bones, and so no one knows where lies the body of good Laurence Sterne. He probably would not have cared, for when death was almost upon him, he said: "I should like another seven or eight months… but be that as it pleases God," and in *Tristram Shandy* he had expressed his desire to die not in his own home, but "in some decent inn," without worrying or bothering his friends. He got his wish in London, where a witness described his last breath: "Now it is come," said Sterne and put up his hand as if to stop a blow.

FUGITIVE WOMEN

Lady Hester Stanhope, the Queen of the Desert

LADY HESTER STANHOPE paid dearly for her satirical talent, although one might also say that she owed both her legend and her reputation to it. The most satisfying period of her life were the years when she lived in and managed the house owned by her uncle, William Pitt the Younger, Prime Minister under George III. Apparently, she proved indispensable, with her arguable beauty, her brilliant, albeit exhausting conversation, and her ability to organize important political supper parties and make them enjoyable. However, her penchant for satire made her so many enemies that when Pitt died in 1806, she found herself surrounded by a great void, though with a full purse: the State gave her a generous life pension, presumably to reward the niece for her extremely loyal uncle's patriotic efforts.

William Pitt wasn't the only man, whether related by blood or not, to have been subjugated by Lady Hester. Although, for her time, she was a giant (she was nearly five foot nine tall), her vitality and talent made her irresistible in her young and not-so-young years, to the extent that it allowed her not to get married. She denied that she was beautiful and claimed that she was possessed, rather, of "a homogeneous ugliness." She was unfortunate in the love of her life, for the famous general, John Moore—upon whom, on the death of her benefactor, her nights and days came to depend—perished in La Coruña during the Peninsular War, or what we Spaniards call the War of Independence.

It was partly this and partly the unbearable loss of power and politicking that drove her to leave England when she was thirty-three, an age which, for a single woman two centuries ago, meant resignation and withdrawal. From that moment on, however, she began to forge the legend of an extremely wealthy woman who travelled incessantly throughout the Middle East with an extravagant and ever-growing entourage—a genuine caravan at certain particularly fruitful periods of her life—with no set goal or aim. Greece, Turkey, Egypt, Lebanon and Syria saw her pass or stay, dressed in Eastern fashion and as a man, surrounded by servants, secretaries, lady companions, hangers-on, French generals fascinated by her personality, or by Dr. Meryon who recorded her escapades, and by her various lovers who were almost always younger and better-looking. Her prestige among the sheikhs and emirs allowed her to travel as far as

Palmyra, a place entirely inaccessible to Westerners at the time. She settled down among the Druses in Mount Lebanon and there, by her own means, exercised the kind of influence which, in her own country, she had failed to inherit from her relations.

It is true that in her witty letters—the main record of her adventures, along with the biographical volumes written by the devoted Meryon—Lady Stanhope was not at all modest or, perhaps, reliable. In one letter, she proclaimed: "I am the oracle of the Arabs and the darling of all the troops who seem to think I am a deity because I can *ride*." And she rode ceaselessly, travelling non-stop and without any apparent objective, plus she sat astride, a style not normally permitted for women in those lands. Lady Hester, however, was a special case, and, in time, she became in part what she claimed to be, for there is nothing like being convinced of something to persuade other people of it too. In her latter years, she was considered to be a fortune-teller or a soothsayer, and her neutrality was immediately sought in any conflict, the adversaries knowing that if she took sides, she could easily take with her many as yet undecided tribes.

In Djoun she had a kind of labyrinthine fortress built, full of pavilions and rooms intended to shelter the illustrious fugitives who would, sooner or later, come asking for asylum, fleeing from the numerous revolutions which she believed were taking place in Europe. She did, in fact, receive a lot of refugees, but none were particularly illustrious or even European: the place became a protective roof for the disinherited and the persecuted of the region.

Lady Hester Stanhope could be charming, but, more often than not, she was quick-tempered and tyrannical, even when being solicitous: she would oblige her visitors to take strange potions and salts to protect them from disease and fever, and sometimes she handed these doses out seven at a time. She smoked a pipe constantly and, during the final months of her life, when she barely left her rooms, it is said that a permanent cloud of smoke emanated from them and that there was not a single object or item of furniture that had not been singed by sparks and cinders. She did not get on well with other women; she boasted that she could tell the character of a man at a single glance; and her indefatigable talk touched on every subject: astrology, the zodiac, philosophy, politics, morality, religion, or literature. She was feared for her mocking burlesques, in particular her imitation of the terrible lisp that afflicted Lord Byron, whom she had met in Athens.

In the final days of her existence, as she lay helpless on her deathbed, she watched as her servants filched everything they could, waiting only for her finally to expire in order to make off with the rest. This was in 1839 when she was sixty-three years old. When her body was found by two Westerners who had come to visit her, they discovered the corpse alone in the fortress: her thirty-seven servants had disappeared and there was nothing left, not even in her bedroom, only the things she was wearing, for no one had dared to touch her. So perhaps she was not lying when she said in another letter: "I am not joking: beneath the triumphal arch of Palmyra, I have been crowned Queen of the Desert."

Vernon Lee, the Tiger-Cat

VERNON LEE WROTE an enormous amount, but, it would seem, poured her real talent into conversation, that ephemeral gift which survivors appropriate so that they can retell, as if they were their own, the anecdotes and witty comments of those who, once dead, can no longer accuse them of plagiarism.

Her real name was Violet Paget, and although she was English by nationality and language, she did not visit London until she was twenty-five. She was born in France and had spent her childhood and adolescence travelling on what her compatriots call "the Continent." What the Paget family practised, though, was not so much travelling as nomadism, changing residence every six months and settling in different parts of Germany, France, Switzerland, Belgium, or Italy. Indeed, all four members of the family prided themselves on never admiring a view, consulting a guidebook or visiting any monument or museum during their travels, and of leading exactly the same life wherever they chose to set up house (they were the declared enemies of tourism), until in 1873, all this racketing around stopped, and they ended up in a villa called "Il Palmerino," near Florence, where Vernon Lee spent most of her adult life.

Her family was clearly not a conventional one; her mother (Vernon Lee's father was her second husband) was a tiny woman, about five feet tall, as despotic as she was lively, irreligious and megalomaniac (she used to make fun of the genealogies in the Bible, but, on the other hand, claimed descent from the kings of France); her relationship with her husband does not appear to have been exactly stimulating, for visitors to the villa often mistook him for the gardener, and his one (infallible) obligation to his wife consisted in accompanying her with a lamp on a night-time walk, after a supper which they always ate separately. As for Vernon or Violet's half-brother, Eugene Lee-Hamilton, eleven years older than her, he had a nervous breakdown in order to avoid a diplomatic transfer to Buenos Aires, and then spent two decades shut up in the house, prostrate on a sofa or a mattress, incapable of moving his limbs, but occasionally writing a few poems.

Although she was not allowed to go out without a chaperone until she was twenty-three, she was precocious as regards literary matters: at thirteen, she published her first piece in a newspaper ("The Biography of a Coin" in French), and at twenty-four, her first book, *Studies of the Eighteenth Century in*

Italy, which astonished readers with what was, for the time, the unusual nature of the subject and with the vast erudition involved. Shortly afterwards, in 1881, she arrived in London and set about consolidating her career by publishing new works and by building personal relationships. With the latter, however, she was unlucky. This is not surprising when one reads the harshness of her judgments and the terrible impression even the most illustrious people made on her: William Morris seemed to her like "a railway porter or a bargee"; she found her teacher, Walter Pater, however much she admired him, "heavy, shy, dull"; she described the painter Whistler as "a mean, nagging, spiteful, sniggling little black thing"; she said that D'Annunzio resembled "an inferior Russian poet. Still I suspect him rather of being—well, a Neapolitan"; and she called Berenson "an ill-tempered and egotistic ass." She thought Oscar Wilde "quite kind," but he avoided her, and as for Henry James, whom she venerated and to whom she dedicated a novel, she had no luck there either: James praised her and took an interest in her work ("She shows prodigious cerebration," he said), but he proved elusive after the publication of a story by Lee in which he quite blatantly appears as a character (her worst sin was not that she should have used him in a story, but that she should have done so without the necessary literary filter). And although James did not deign to read the story himself, references to it were enough for him to warn his philosopher brother William in a letter: "…she is as dangerous and uncanny as she is intelligent—which is saying a great deal. Her vigour and sweep of intellect are most rare and her talk superior altogether… At any rate draw it mild with her on the question of friendship. She's a tiger-cat!"

Most of Vernon Lee's friendships were female and, on her part, rather obsessive, although they were, it seems, based entirely on a communion of intellects, which means that hers overwhelmed the intellects of those friends. When she found out that one of them was getting married to a man whom she had met only three times, she suffered a nervous collapse which was only the first in a series of such attacks that would last until her death. Another friend said that when she saw her for the first time, she felt like the Virgin before the Angel of the Annunciation. Vernon Lee must have been entirely asexual: she certainly never married and there was no mention of any love affair, and she was quite clear on the subject: "Loving people in the way of being willing to do anything for them is *intolerable* to me. I *cannot* like, or love, at the expense of having my skin rubbed off. I can do without people. I find it more comfortable to do without them."

She wore suits, occasionally a tie, occasionally a soft felt hat, and glasses that toned down her fiery grey-green eyes—the eyes of a "tigress," according to another female friend. Her lower lip and her teeth were rather protuberant, her nose ungrateful: she said of herself that she had "a baroque ugliness." Her talk was brilliant, her wit caustic, and she came up with so many arguments in a discussion that she would sometimes contradict herself and it would become hard to follow her. Her many original studies on aesthetics are now rather antiquated and her novels were never very good, but her books on the "spirit of place" and, in particular, her stories about ghosts or the supernatural are written with a mastery that approaches that of Isak Dinesen.

At the end of her life, she read Freud, but got nothing from him: she considered him an obscurantist, her bête noire. She died in 1935, at the age of seventy-eight. During her final years, she could hear nothing, and so spent those years even more isolated from the world than she always had been, and lacking the two things she most enjoyed, conversation, at which she excelled, and music, which consoled her.

ADAH ISAACS MENKEN, THE
EQUESTRIAN POETESS

IT SEEMS ODD that at the end of her vertiginous life, Adah
Isaacs Menken's main concern should have been the publication
of her one book of poems entitled *Infelicia*, which, in fact, she
never saw, because she died on August 10, 1868, just a week
before it appeared. It is true, however, that during the dozen or so
years when she was at her most famous, she was not indifferent to
literature or to men of letters, although she spent most of her

time on stage, tied to a horse, and it was more because of this and the continuous scandals linked to her name that she became the first internationally known American lady of the theatre and a favourite of newspapers on two continents.

Many of her contemporaries questioned the words "lady" and "theatre" when applied to her. As well as her four husbands (who included a boxer and a gambler – the latter came to a sticky end in Denver), she had numerous lovers, some of whom, inevitably, were writers, such as Alexandre Dumas *père* at the end of his days and that masochistic poet par excellence, Algernon Charles Swinburne, that tiny, red-haired, Victorian, homosexual drunkard, addicted to the whip. Adah Isaacs Menken had dealings of a different sort with other writers too: Walt Whitman was her friend and she was his first disciple; George Sand was godmother to her first child, the magnificently named Louis Dudevant Victor Emmanuel, who lived but briefly; the ill-fated Fitz-James O'Brien, a friend of Poe and possibly just as talented, was her companion in revels; Charles Dickens, when he was an easy-going, respectable gentleman, gave his permission for The Menken (as she herself liked to be called) to dedicate her slender volume of poems to him; Gautier praised her during his stay in Paris; Verlaine mocked her in a few malicious verses; and, as for her compatriot Mark Twain, when he was still Samuel Clemens, he bequeathed to posterity the most complete description of her performances. Menken's art, alas, failed to impress that Southern journalist and, alas for her, Clemens was to make his name as a satirist. Adah Menken's pièce de résistance, the one that made her famous in half the world, was the ride at the end of *Mazeppa*, an extremely free adaptation of Byron's play, in which she played the eponymous hero. For all Twain's malevolence, it is clear that the star's interpretative gifts were nothing if not original: on one occasion, she played Lady Macbeth and—quite involuntarily and without the audience even noticing—changed Shakespeare's text (in these more classical perform-ances, her fellow actors, less gifted in improvisation, were, thanks to her, left floundering). The reason people went to see her in *Mazeppa*, however, was her final appearance on stage tied to the back of the horse and wearing a skin-tight, flesh-coloured leotard which, even from a short distance away, creat-ed the illusion that the actress was naked (it mattered little that The Menken was also sporting a ridiculous little moustache in keeping with her masculine role). According to Twain, who regretted not having taken his binoculars to the theatre, Menken appeared to be wearing not a leotard but "a thin, tight, white linen garment, of unimportant dimensions; I forget the name of the article, but it is indispensable to infants of tender age." He considered the actress-hero's behaviour throughout the performance as "lunatic," and was pleased that in the second most popular play in her repertoire, *The French Spy*, The Menken played the part "as dumb as an oyster," and so her "extravagant gesticulations" seemed almost passable.

If we are to believe her chronicler, it seems inexplicable that an actress of such limited scope should for years have been able to fill theatres on both sides of the Atlantic. She must have had other qualities too. In person, she was doubtless a great seductress, capable of taming and even charming her most acerbic critics, among them the journalist Newell, who was utterly scathing about her, but who ended up being her husband for a week (another husband lasted only three days). And it would seem that her talent for provocation and publicity had no equal in the world until well into the twentieth century. When Baltimore was about to fall to the Union during the Civil War, she decided to remember her roots (she had been born near New Orleans and may have been a quadroon) and demanded that the entire theatre be painted grey to match the uniforms of the Confederate troops who were about to lose the city; when she had time (for she also gave lectures), she revealed herself to be one of the bravest, wisest, and most ironic feminists of her day, protesting against the enslavement of women and always doing exactly as she pleased, until she was arrested by Northern troops. As she wrote in a letter: "They wanted to send me to 'Dixie,' but would not permit me to take but one hundred pounds of luggage. Of course I could not see that... I wasn't going across the lines without any clothes."

We know little about the true facts of her life and a great deal about its legends: it was even said that she was a Spanish Jewess born in Madrid (she may well have been Jewish), who, in her adolescence, had been a prostitute in Havana (having first been corrupted by an Austrian baron) and that, when she was famous, she appeared before the Emperor Franz Josef, at the court of Vienna, wearing a cape which she removed on greeting him to reveal, underneath, the equestrian costume she wore in *Mazeppa*, the one that gave every appearance of nudity (she did not, apparently, take the horse to the palace). There are numerous photos of her, almost always in *poses plastiques*, and the most delightful of these is one that shows her sitting on the knee of an old, fat and almost shirtless Dumas, with her head resting on his convex chest.

Although she suffered more than a few falls from her horse, one of which occurred shortly before her death, she seems to have died of something else, although the doctors could not agree as to what this was, nor did they seem very interested in doing so. It is not entirely clear when she was born, but she was, at the time, in her thirties: in her final years she became increasingly depressed, absorbed in writing about the character of Shylock and, as I said at the start, worrying, above all, about her poems. However, rumour has it that it was her own fault that she did not see the published volume, being too preoccupied with choosing which portrait of her should adorn the cover, changing her mind again and again, thus delaying her launch as a poetess for so long that the book, in the end, was published posthumously. Perhaps it was for the best, since, although she had long ago ceased caring what the critics said about her performances, the virulent reviews that her poetry received might have wounded her deeply.

Violet Hunt, the Improper Person of Babylon

NO ONE COULD ever have accused Violet Hunt of being consistent, at least as regards her love life, for while she had a great liking for "irregular situations," she also suffered frequent and spectacular attacks of respectability. The worst of these attacks occurred during her relationship with that famous man of letters, Ford Madox Ford, author of the brilliant novel *The Good Soldier* and close friend and collaborator of Conrad. Faced by his wife's refusal to grant him a divorce and by Hunt's insistence on ceasing to be merely his lover, Ford was on the point of retrieving the German citizenship of his ancestors in order to be able to marry under German law, and even underwent a depressing simulacrum of marriage, with a defrocked priest officiating, all in order to please his unhappy mistress. The result of this whole operation was scandal and a law suit—with the two Mrs. Fords in the middle—which brought the novelist a few days in prison and Violet Hunt both a brief period of exile in Europe and the displeasure of one of the men she most admired, the very cautious and formal Henry James, who described the situation as "lamentable, lamentable, oh, lamentable!"

Violet Hunt was another of his protegées, with all of whom, contrary to the usual implications of the term, James had only the most chaste of relationships. Not that there was, in this case, any lack of opportunity, for, on one occasion, when invited to James's house in the country, Violet fell ill after supper and threw up. She took advantage of the situation to go and change and presented herself in the living room later dressed only in a Chinese robe and, as she puts it in her diaries, "in a flirtatious mood." James, however, began a long disquisition on the novels of Mrs. Humphry Ward, whom it seems, he read more and valued more highly than he did Violet, who, to her double chagrin, never became a Mrs.

James was not the first older man with whom Violet had tried her luck: when she was thirteen, she had offered herself in marriage to that apostle of the aesthetic, John Ruskin, who was, at the time, fifty-six. She felt terribly sorry for him after the death of Rose La Touche, for whom Ruskin had long yearned, having been captivated by her when she was just ten years old: a patient man, he had had the good taste to wait until she was eighteen, only to be met with rejection and, years afterwards, her death. Fortunately for Violet, her generous offer was also postponed and, later, forgotten. It seems that even the young Oscar Wilde—when his sexuality was more all-embracing—proposed marriage to her, and we know that Violet was one of the few women who succeeded in seducing an ingenuous and subsequently far more restrained Somerset Maugham, while she herself was seduced by H.G. Wells, a well-known womaniser. One should not infer from the mention of all these famous names that Violet Hunt was a megalomaniac, for some of her most difficult and enduring affairs were with men who have not passed into history, such as the diplomat who not only had five or six other lovers besides her, but also infected her with syphilis. Before that, another man had brought her both pain and pleasure, a man only three years younger than her father and, like him, a painter.

The most striking thing about all this is, without a doubt, the era itself, for, having been born in 1862, Violet Hunt not only enjoyed to the full the brief Edwardian reign of great permissiveness (as long as any "irregularities" were not found out), she lived through much of the prim Victorian era too. This means, by the way, that Violet Hunt was forty-six when she began her affair with Ford Madox Ford, who was eleven years her junior. In those days it was a rare woman who could boast of having found the love of her life at such an age. One can only assume that Violet, though mature in years, was still rather ingenuous, since she fell into Ford's trap in a somewhat theatrical manner: "by the will of Providence," according to her (but it seems that it was more thanks to a timely nudge from him), her hand slipped into Ford's jacket pocket and in it discovered a bottle, bearing the label on which was scrawled the word "POISON." She snatched the bottle from him and asked if he had been intending to drink the stuff. He said that he had and she, judging that she had saved his life, felt duty bound to love him. Those who knew the real Mrs. Ford said that, in the same situation, she would probably have encouraged her husband to drink it.

In the midst of all this passion, Violet Hunt still found time for many other things, such as supporting the suffragist movement, avoiding being propositioned by well-known lesbians, attending a thousand and one parties, and writing articles and books, thirty-one of the latter, including novels, stories, poems, plays, and translations. Those that have best survived are her neo-Gothic tales and her ghost stories, which are truly splendid, and which Henry James suggested should be entitled (although she, alas, refused) *Ghost Stories by a Woman of the World*, which, of course, she was, so much so that one has the feeling sometimes that her admiring colleagues loved her and kept up with her more for her inexhaustible abilities as a gossip and as an opener of social doors than for her literary gifts. She was always looking for patrons, but only managed to find rather half-hearted and reluctant ones in James and Conrad and Wells and Hudson. The first of these, much given to nicknames, used to refer to her either as "the Improper Person of Babylon" or "his Purple Patch," because of the colour of the hat and coat she was wearing the first time he met her.

She had no lovers after Ford and, at the end of her life, she went in for creating, without much success, scheming, treacherous male characters. Advancing syphilis affected her mind and caused her to make some irreparable faux-pas: she once said to the novelist Michael Arlen: "Michael Arlen's really quite a nice young man—and extremely clever. I wonder why it is that his books are so *awful*." It is no wonder that she became progressively lonelier and sadder until her death in 1942, at the age of seventy-nine. Her strong, contradictory personality survives in a few memorable characters created by those more important writers who were her friends or lovers: she inspired them, but they did not manage to make her very happy. Only a very naïve person could say that they, in exchange, immortalised her.

Julie de Lespinasse, the Amorous Mistress

THE LIFE OF Julie de Lespinasse was short, painful, and complicated, which only makes her extraordinary capacity for bringing people together and putting them at their ease all the more commendable. Those who attended the long daily gatherings in her salon in Rue de Bellechasse (among them D'Alembert the

encyclopedist, Diderot, Condorcet, Marmontel, prelates, noble-
men, diplomats, and ladies of all kinds, even the wives of field
marshals) bear witness to her remarkable ability to keep magisterial control over these meetings of privileged minds and
demanding intellects, even though she herself barely contributed to the conversation. It is no wonder, then, that when her
protectress Madame du Deffand threw her out of her house,
accusing her of betraying her and of appropriating her friends,
most of those now mutual friends, forced to choose between the
two salons, opted to follow the less witty but more agreeable of
the two ladies. Such was the feeling of harmony that she managed to create among her guests that, on the death of their host-
ess, one of them, Monsieur de Guibert, put it very succinctly:
"We have been sundered." Indeed, they saw no further reason to
continue meeting, knowing that they would not be the same people without her presence.

Julie de Lespinasse's origins were murky and unpromising;
she was the illegitimate daughter of the Comtesse d'Albon, and
no one knows with absolute certainty who her father was,
although it seems likely that it was the Comte de Vichy,
Madame du Deffand's elder brother. The Comtesse d'Albon
had another legitimate daughter, who, in time (in 1739), married Vichy, who thus became the brother-in-law of his unac-
knowledged daughter, as well as the husband of his niece and
ex-lover of his mother-in-law. None of this proved of much
help to Julie de Lespinasse when that mother-in-law, her mother, died: she went to live with her double relatives, who treated
her like a servant or worse, until Madame du Deffand (who was,
I suppose, both aunt and sister-in-law) took pity on her and
decided to sweep her off to Paris, with the aforementioned
results. Julie herself, who was always discreet as to her origins,
confessed, nevertheless, that nothing could surprise her in the

convoluted novels of Richardson and Prévost, so full of consanguineous complications, and that may be why her favourite author was Sterne, whom she deciphered, imitated, and possibly received as a guest on one of his Paris trips.

Her life, however, was more like something out of *Pamela* or *Manon Lescaut* than *Tristram Shandy*, and if Julie de Lespinasse has passed into history it is, as with her protectress and rival, because of her letters. These two sets of correspondence could not be more different: if Madame du Deffand was noted for her pessimism, her caustic humour and her scepticism, Mademoiselle de Lespinasse was all ardour and passion, at least in most of the letters that have survived, those addressed to Monsieur de Guibert, whom she loved regretfully and frenziedly and rather belatedly. Before that, she had loved, with fewer regrets but just as frenziedly, a brilliant Spaniard, the Marqués de Mora, of whom all his contemporaries said he was unworthy of Spain—as continues to be the case today, for any compatriot with the slightest degree of talent is invariably mistreated. Mora, who once wrote her twenty-two letters while he was away for ten days in Fontainebleau, had to leave Paris for health reasons; he returned, then had to leave again, but this time he did not return, for he died in Bordeaux in 1774. Even before his death, however, Julie de Lespinasse had already met Monsieur de Guibert, who was, at the time, a 29-year-old colonel, so charming that ladies even took the trouble to read his one book, a rather dry work entitled *Essai de tactique*, about which they would exclaim: *"Oh, Monsieur de Guibert, que votre tic-tac est admirable!"* Inevitably, Julie de Lespinasse, who was almost in her forties by then, was not the only woman in Guibert's life; indeed, in the end, the colonel went so far as to marry another woman without this in any way diminishing the love and devotion of the fiery Mademoiselle Julie. Her letters to the flighty soldier are, without a doubt, among the great literary monuments that women of talent have, with relative frequency, erected to total good-for-nothings.

And yet, perhaps the saddest character in this story is Monsieur d'Alembert, the great encyclopedist. For many years, he lived with Mademoiselle de Lespinasse, apparently on chaste terms that had not always (that is, before they lived together) been observed. Whatever the truth of the matter, he was convinced that he was the prime object of his great friend's thoughts, as doubtless she was of his, Encyclopaedia apart of course. On her death, he discovered that Julie had appointed him her executor and he, to his misfortune, had to go through her papers: not a single one of his letters had been preserved, whereas Mora's many tons of correspondence were all there. Distraught, he went in search of Guibert (who received many letters, but probably did not reply) and said: "We were all wrong! It was Mora she loved!" Needless to say, in those polite times, Guibert remained silent. D'Alembert survived her by seven years, during which time he accepted lodging in the Louvre, in his role as secretary of the Académie Française. He was inconsolable, and when his friend Marmontel reminded him of his late beloved's behaviour, he replied: "Yes, she had changed, but I had not; she no longer lived for me, but I always lived for her; now that she is no longer here, I have no reason to live. What is left to me now? When I go home, instead of her, I find her shadow. These rooms in the Louvre are like a tomb; I never enter them without a shudder of horror."

Julie de Lespinasse had died on May 23, 1776, at the age of forty-three, surrounded by her closest friends. During her last three days, she was so weak that she could barely speak. The nurses revived her with cordials and made her sit up for a moment in bed. And her last words were of surprise. "Still alive?" she said.

EMILY BRONTË, THE SILENT MAJOR

THE LIFE OF Emily Brontë was so short and silent and is now so remote that very little is known about her, not that this has stopped her biographer compatriots from retelling her life in fat and usually rather vacuous volumes. Although there are, as far as history is concerned, always three Brontë sisters, there were, in fact, five, to whom, as people all too frequently forget, one should also add their brother Branwell, who, however disastrous and alcoholic he may have been, was nonetheless important in the life of the most famous of the sisters. The two sisters no one ever mentions were called Maria and Elizabeth, and they died from tuberculosis, one after the other, when they were still children. In a rather Dickensian episode, they were harshly treated by their teachers shortly before they died, being punished and insulted and forced to get out of bed when they were already ill. Posterity has laid a strange reproach at Emily's door: namely, that, despite being the school favourite, she failed to intercede for the victims, and remained silent before this rank injustice. The reproach is particularly unfair given that the author of *Wuthering Heights* was not yet six years old, five and four years younger, respectively, than her two ill-treated sisters. After them came Charlotte and then Branwell, and after Emily, Anne, the youngest, the three surviving sisters all becoming novelists, while Branwell became merely a frustrated poet. Their mother had died when Emily was three years old, and they were all brought up by their Irish-born father, who, as a writer of sermons, was not unconnected with literature himself. Other less pious members of the family initiated the sisters into the oral tradition, with the Irish story-tellers' habitual preference for tales of ghosts and demons and goblins. This was doubtless Emily's first contact with the supernatural, which hovers over her one novel from first page to last.

Her silence apparently caused her more than one upset and gave her a reputation for arrogance: from adolescence on, Emily would often answer only in monosyllables or not at all, which caused some people to shun her and drew protests from her sisters. She was, however, her father's favourite, as demonstrated by the fact that he taught her how to fire a pistol and often took her out target shooting (to which she became addicted). Mr. Brontë—who exoticised his original name of Brunty when he was studying (where else?) at Oxford (perhaps because *bronte* means "thunder" in Greek)—was thought to be eccentric and austere and, although these extant reports come from rather unreliable sources (that is, sources with an axe to grind), it is said that, in his zeal, he refused to give his daughters meat to eat and condemned them to a diet of potatoes; they say that one rainy night, after he had discovered that the girls were wearing dainty boots given to them by a friend, he burned the boots because he deemed them too luxurious; he tore to shreds a silk dress that his wife kept in a trunk, more to look at than to wear; and, on one occasion, he sawed the backs off various chairs to make them into stools. If all this is true, then the Brontë sisters did very well in not turning to drink like their brother. And regardless of whether or not it is true, one thing is clear, Mr. Brontë was also extremely affectionate towards them and, indeed, took the trouble to educate them: he would have them put on masks and would then interrogate them, believing that, with their faces covered, they would become used to responding freely and boldly. He once asked Emily what he should do with Branwell when he was at his most impossible: "Reason with him, and when he won't listen to reason, whip him." She was six years old at the time, and clearly had a proclivity for drastic measures. When she was older, she punched her dog Keeper in the face and eyes—they swelled right up—to stop the dog from going for her throat after she had reprimanded him. On another occasion, she separated the same dog and a stray, with whom it had become embroiled in a fight, by sprinkling pepper on their snouts, which indicates that, despite her silence, she was a very decisive woman. It was no coincidence that her sisters nicknamed her "The Major." Nevertheless, and despite being the tallest in the family, she was sometimes described as rather a fragile creature with precarious health. After a stay of eight months with her sisters in Belgium, there were also some fears for her mental health, but that is a fairly commonplace accusation in family disputes. She loved Walter Scott and was a devotee of both Shelley and the night, which is why she slept very little, in order to enjoy it to the full.

It was her sister Charlotte who, not without great difficulty, managed to persuade her to publish her poems. Later on, all three sisters, under the pseudonyms Currer, Ellis and Acton Bell, sent their respective first novels to the publishers. The only one that was not, initially, accepted was Charlotte's, but her second novel, *Jane Eyre*, was. The reviews of *Wuthering Heights* were very positive, but no one dared hail it as the masterpiece that time has shown it to be.

In 1848, a year after its publication, Emily often had to go to the Black Bull Inn to fetch Branwell and help him back home. Her concern was merely routine, and neither she, through lack of foresight, nor Charlotte, out of a spirit of revenge, did anything serious about curing Branwell, who went to his grave not long afterwards, having spent periods racked by horrific coughing fits and terrible insomnia. Emily followed him only three months later, and although a housemaid declared that "Miss Emily died of a broken heart for love of her brother," giving rise to speculations about incest, it is more likely that Emily Brontë knew nothing in life of the passions she so skilfully described in her semi-incestuous *Wuthering Heights*.

During her illness, she refused to have any treatment or to be seen by a doctor and once again plunged into long silences, prepared to let nature take its course, although nature proved far from benign. On December 19, she insisted on leaving her bed and getting dressed, then she sat down by the fire in her room and started combing her long, abundant tresses. Her comb fell into the flames, and since she did not have the strength to pick it up, the bedroom was filled with the smell of burning bone. Afterwards, she went down to the living room and there, sitting on the sofa, she died at two o'clock in the afternoon, having refused to go back to bed. She was only thirty years old and she wrote nothing more.

PERFECT ARTISTS

NO ONE KNOWS what Cervantes looked like, and no one knows for certain what Shakespeare looked like either, and so *Don Quixote* and *Macbeth* are both texts unaccompanied by a personal expression, a definitive face or a gaze which, over time, the eyes of other men have been able to freeze and make their own. Or perhaps only those that posterity has felt the need to bestow on them, with a great deal of hesitation, bad conscience, and unease—an expression, gaze, and face that were undoubtedly not those of Shakespeare or of Cervantes.

It is as if the books we still read felt more alien and incomprehensible without some image of the heads that composed them; it is as if our age, in which everything has its corresponding image, felt uncomfortable with something whose authorship cannot be attributed to a face; it is almost as if a writer's features formed part of his or her work. Perhaps the authors of the last two centuries anticipated this and so left behind them numerous portraits, in paintings and in photographs, which may be why, over the years, I have got into the habit of collecting postcards of those portraits. This collection, entirely unmethodical and merely accumulative, now comprises about one hundred and fifty images. These are the ones I am accustomed to seeing, those with which I am familiar. It is these portraits, and no others (possibly better or more striking), with which I identify and always will identify Dickens, Faulkner or Rilke, because I have them to hand and occasionally look at them. It is significant that there is not a single Spaniard among them, but I have the impression that in Spain we are not interested in this kind of image, for there are no picture postcards of Spanish writers, or at least, I have never managed to find any. In England it is exactly the opposite, given that London has a museum—the National Portrait Gallery—devoted entirely to portraits, and from which, inevitably, many of these faces come. In this essay, I will limit myself to looking at them once again, briefly, not at all of them, just a few, but now with my pen in my hand. It would be naïve to try and extract from them lessons or laws, or even common characteristics. The only thing that leaps out at one is that all the subjects are writers and now, at last, when they are all dead, all of them are perfect artists.

One might, however, observe that very few of these post-cards show the whole figure of the writer; indeed, few of them show much more than the writer's isolated head, as if the words by which we know them had emerged only from there and not also from their hands. Of the few who are shown seated or even lying down or standing—thus revealing, partially or complete-ly, their generally irrelevant bod-ies—Dickens is perhaps the most extraordinary, even though his poses seem fairly unstudied and everyday. The author must have posed, but might not have done so. On all three occasions he is seated, and in two of the photos, he is seated astride a chair, facing the chair-back. In the first one of him alone, one might think the posture artificial, rehearsed. He is leaning

his arms on the back of the chair, with his right arm raised so that his head, gracefully and melancholically inclined, is resting on that hand. His gaze is self-consciously dreamy, but it also has a look of steel, as if he were witnessing some disagreeable spectacle. The slightly tousled hair, the goatee beard, the not too creased trousers. In the second photo he is with his daughters, reading to them from far too slender a tome for it to be one of his own books. Here, too, he is sitting astride the chair, facing the chair-back, and such a coincidence inevitably makes one think that Dickens must, in fact, *almost always* have sat like that. In this second photo his hair and beard are greyer and more kempt, and you can see his rather small

feet, and the clothes he is wearing are more informal. In both portraits, he is sitting very erect, as if he were rather short or, perhaps, nervous. In both, contrary to one's expectations, he looks serious, he does not seem a jolly man, or even happy, but rather prickly and dapper. His daughters worship him, adore him, put up with his every whim and tantrum. There is something of the dandy about him, but he does not deceive us: the man who gave life to Pickwick, Micawber, Weller, Snodgrass and to so many others reveals his true witty, jocular self in that one detail: he is a man who does not mind posing with his legs unceremoniously akimbo, he is a man who sits astride chairs.

He is not doing so in the third photo, in which, nevertheless, he again reveals his intelligence and astuteness, for he is not pretending to be writing, which would be both vulgar and difficult to do, instead, he is pretending to be *thinking* with his pen in his hand, and with both pen and hand resting on the paper. Dickens has paused to ponder the next sentence, a sentence he will not write, with his eyes abstracted and slightly amused, which is hardly surprising, given that the last thing we could believe of him, or that, doubtless, he could believe of himself, is that he would ever stop to think for that length of time when writing his vast, helter-skelter novels.

Mallarmé is holding a pen which does not touch the paper, and he, therefore, *is* pretending to be writing, but he does it very badly, with his folded shawl about his shoulders, the desk before him set against a telltale blank wall. Unlike Dickens, who manages to distance himself from and to dominate the camera, Mallarmé is not only dependent on it, he is fascinated and enslaved. For him that moment is an eternal moment, a self-confessedly historic performance, and his look is that of someone who has already received or is still obligingly awaiting instructions, a look of obedience, gratitude, and childish excitement. The

man behind that gaze feels a naïve sense of wonderment at progress, as he might wonder at a sonnet with a rhyme ending in -yx. That is why the oil painting by Manet is much more real-

istic, here a cigar replaces the pen, and the left hand—which, in the photo, merely awaits the coming of the eternal moment and does not quite know what to do—is hidden in his jacket pocket in what has all the appearance of being an habitual gesture. In the painting, Mallarmé is younger and thinner, he leans back easily and is not looking at anything: he does not yet believe in the existence of eternal moments.

Oscar Wilde, on the other hand, always believed in them and only in them, which is why, one by one, he nurtures them. His capacity for dressing up is so extreme that, in the end, the disguise becomes utterly authentic, the thing we notice least and which is of least importance. What most concerns him is his own face, and in both portraits Wilde yearns *to be* a handsome man and manages to

look as if he really was: the way models in advertisements do now. The expression of the mouth is the same on both occasions, as if its owner knew full well, from looking at himself in the mirror, that it is the only acceptable one, the only flattering one. The odd thing about the two photos is that all Wilde's irony and humour have gone into his clothes and are entirely absent from his face, which takes itself very seriously indeed. The flared nostrils indicate that Wilde is waiting, holding his breath. He is a man who, despite everything, is convinced that beauty can come only from the face and from its expression. He doesn't really care about the ring, the cane, the long hair, the gloves, the furs, the hat, the cape, and the cravat tied in a bow, they are merely the initial and subsequently dispensable lure, the thing that will make the viewer notice his photos, a necessary requisite if the viewer is then to notice what is truly important, the gaze and face of someone who, beyond all the jokes, wishes to achieve, above all, the beauty of seriousness.

This is not something that appears to worry Baudelaire, perhaps because he has such noble features that he does not need to. When he is younger and has more hair, he looks shifty, his hands in his pockets, and, when he is older and balder, he looks angry or expectant—impatient. He has a natural elegance, even more so with age, and he has, too, an air of deliberation; and the ear that appears in both photos is quite remarkable, its sharpness underlining the intensity of the whole image, as do the lines that will later become wrinkles. The

expression is almost identical in both portraits, harder and more disgruntled in the second, like someone who wants to get things over with and who is already thinking about what cannot and will not appear in the image, about what is outside any image. He is, above all, a man in a hurry; even while he is being photographed, he has already disappeared, perhaps because what animates him is not apparent in his face, is not contained by his face.

The same can be said of Henry James, even when he wore a beard, in his already extremely bald youth. That hirsute image

is certainly not the one that has survived, but the one in Sargent's painting, which is very like that in the photo taken with his older brother William. James's face is a uniform whole, the cheeks and cranium forming the indivisible continuum of a politician or a banker. However, in the Sargent painting with its opaque gaze, there is one detail that undermines this apparent respectability and precludes him

from being either politician or banker: the thumb hooked in his waistcoat pocket, clumsily or timidly, uncomfortable and ill at ease, the whole awkward hand hanging from there. In the photo, on the other hand, only his eyes save him from being passed over, that and the jolly bow tie, an extraordinary concession to fantasy in such an ascetic person. But

the gaze is frighteningly intelligent, for it is an intelligence turned outwards, far more inquisitive than that of his philosopher brother, whose face, at first glance, seems, erroneously, to have more personality: you have only to look at their eyes to see this, William looks straight ahead, almost without seeing, Henry is looking to one side, doubtless seeing even what is not there.

Sterne's gaze leaves no room for doubt: in a century replete with lively gazes, it is one of the liveliest, and it belongs to a man conscious of his great talent, yet without being vain. In Reynolds' portrait, he shows his hands with utter naturalness, the index finger of his right hand resting on his forehead, pointing to his intellect, the left resting on one thigh, comfortable, sure of itself and of the rightness of that position, so different from the photograph of Mallarmé. He is blithely crushing with his elbow the very pages for which he will be remembered (he will be above them for as long as he lives), and on his lips there is just the beginning of a sweetly malevolent smile, the smile of someone who knows what he is going to say the moment his companion stops speaking, for he seems to be listening courteously (awaiting his turn) to someone less skilled in rhetoric. The marble bust, on the other hand, is a failed idealization: the Roman coiffure and the incongruous nakedness are belied by those

eyes like two burning coals and by the enormous nose: he looks the exact opposite of a man in repose, indeed, it looks as if that face could never rest, not even while imprisoned in a block of marble, which, despite everything, is filled by his agitated breathing.

Gide, like James, has his thumb hooked in his waistcoat pocket, but the gesture here gives off a very different, almost contrary signal. In this young Gide, wearing beard, cape, and hat, there is a good deal of swagger and a clear inclination toward aggression; he looks almost like a professional duellist. His eyes are mean, elusive, and disdainful, and everything about him (the raised collar, the beard, the determined stance) is sharp and bristling. Miraculously, almost all of these qualities have disappeared in the photo taken in his maturity: in it one sees a sad, sympathetic man, any hardness evident only in those thin, clearly outlined lips and contradicted by the generous eyebrows and by the glasses that soften a possibly sorrowful and apparently commisera-

tive gaze. If you look at each photo separately, you will find yourself in both cases before a mysterious man, however much of himself he set down in his diaries. If you look at them both at once, you will find yourself before an enigma.

Conrad, whom Gide translated, sits, looking very serious, in an armchair, not knowing where to put his hands, which is why one of them is clenched and the other open, covering and concealing the first. He is very concerned about his appearance, as if he were a man who did not normally dress as well as this, that is, not as immaculately as he is here. His portrait is intended to be a monument to respectability, which emigrants

and exiles go to such lengths to obtain, for they must, above all, show that they are decent people. His beard is meticulously trimmed, but it could hardly be that of a genuine English citizen, with that tapering, triangular shape and that moustache with its pointed ends. His lashless eyes are very severe, they could be those of a just man nursing his anger, of an innocent man being judged. Or perhaps they are merely the eyes of an Oriental.

Although not Oriental, William Faulkner's eyes belong to the same family, and, in the photo, he, too, is all dressed up, like the best man at a wedding, thanks to that insolently protuberant handkerchief and his perfectly groomed, very white hair. With

his furrowed brow, he gives the impression that he has reluctantly abandoned the idea of shooting the man about to become his son-in-law and has resigned himself to seeing him transformed into precisely that, but this decision is so recent that in his left hand you can still see a trace of the gesture of someone who could quite calmly

and determinedly pick up a rifle. In the second photo, Faulkner is scratching his shirt-sleeved arm and is surrounded by tiny dogs, but the photo lacks all informality, nor is it in any way idyllic or even peaceful: his profile is as severe as his forehead is in the first photo, the back of his neck neatly shaven, a timid, even unsociable man. In both instances he looks like someone who has just noticed the arrival of some bothersome, inopportune visitors to whom he does

not even wish to speak. Faulkner would doubtless prefer to stay with his dogs or go straight to his daughter's wedding, even if he does have to leave his rifle behind.

Poor Borges seems so patient and full of regret: he is fifty-three years old and is sitting on a stool and has taken off his glasses, not out of vanity, but to help the work of the photographer, to whom one should always offer an unobstructed face. He is holding them, very provisionally, in his hands. He is someone without guile, almost innocent, apparently helpless. He does not know that sitting on a stool requires either an upright posture or nonchalantly crossed legs, nor that any recently removed spectacles should, at the very least, be hidden from the camera, nor that a buttoned-up jacket (which is, I

would say, reddish-brown in colour) is too great a sign of probity. He is smartly dressed, but rather as if he had been photographed on a Sunday. And his eyes, as a result of that suddenly recovered myopia, tell us what we know to have been their fate: without glasses, they cannot see, not, of course, that this stops them looking.

Rilke does not have the face one would suppose him to have, so delicate and unbearable was he in his habits and needs as a great poet when he wrote, vanquishing habits and fulfilling needs. His face is frankly dangerous, with those dark circles under deep-set eyes, and the sparse, drooping moustache which gives him a strangely Mongolian appearance; those cold, oblique eyes make him look almost cruel, and only his hands—clasped as they should be, unlike Conrad's indecisive hands—and the quality of his clothes—an excellent tie and excellent cloth—give him some semblance of repose or somewhat mitigate that cruelty. The truth is that he could be a visionary doctor in his laboratory, awaiting the results of some mon-

strous and forbidden experiment.

Poor, wretched Poe, on the other hand, seems entirely inoffensive, despite the baleful look, domed forehead and thin, unkempt hair: he has one hand tucked inside his jacket, as if he were Napoleon, but in order to do this, he has had to undo no fewer than four buttons on his waistcoat; he looks like a bum. He may, of course, think he is putting on a

good front: an innocent in threadbare clothes, but they are the best he has.

He doubtless belongs to the same lineage as unkempt Nietzsche, who holds what looks like a coachman's hat in his left hand and, on his other arm, his mother, whom he has not yet

learned to see as a disagreeable woman, and for whom he still feels respect, if not something more. Nietzsche's hair is as dishevelled as his moustache, and his overcoat looks as if it had been lent to him by some much burlier relative. In the other photo, of him alone, he looks more groomed, his overcoat fits better, his moustache is more tamed and his hair less wild. However, his rather damp-looking hair sticks up a little too much, as if he had pushed it back from his forehead for a moment, the moment required for the photo to

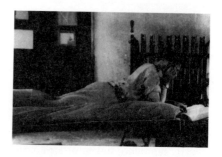

be taken. His right hand is pressed against his cheek, and his face is that of someone rushing forward at high speed: it is as if his composure were held together with pins.

T.E. Lawrence does not, on the whole, look very composed when he is not being Lawrence of Arabia, but a soldier in the RAF called Ross or Shaw, so different from the idealized image of him in paintings, wearing his disguise. Without it, he doesn't know how to stand, his chin on his hand, that hand on his upright arm, that elbow on his other hand, that hand closed, and all this when he is standing up. In the first photo, looking rather diminutive and wearing too-short trousers, he reminds one of Stan Laurel, while, in the second, his skinny legs and puny chest inspire our pity, and again we see a hand appear in the strangest of places, to achieve which he has had to twist his arm round behind him. His features are plebeian, the features of the person he wanted to be: a soldier, a proletarian. In the third photo, he is lying on his camp bed reading, with the back of his neck exposed, one of those rare moments of non-suffering, those moments which he did not perhaps describe in his book *The Mint*.

Djuna Barnes, with her coat over her shoulders and her beautiful turban, is the most distinguished figure in the gallery.

She is conscientiously posing and has dressed conscientiously, but in her this merely reproduces her daily custom. Unlike Wilde, who tried to be and to seem handsome, she knows she is not pretty and does not believe she can seem so, that is why she makes no attempt to adopt the faraway look that flatters most faces, instead she looks straight ahead, skeptical and

mocking, trusting only in her costume (especially that raised coat collar) and in the confidence of the pose. The necklace does not adorn her, it protects her. She is a woman dominated far more by modesty than by esteem for her own image.

Mark Twain and Nabokov were not modest at all; rather, they were histrionic. The former, in shirt or nightshirt, is writing in bed, and in his case, one can only think that, unlike Mallarmé or Dickens, he is not pretending, but really is diligently writing a word, for he is not a man to waste time. He could not possibly have been unaware that he was being photographed, but that is the impression he gives, that he neither knows nor cares. The bed is tidy, it does not look like the bed of someone ill, for the bed of an invalid is always sunken and untidy, the pillows flat.

Thus, the viewer can only wonder if perhaps Mark Twain spent his entire life in bed.

As for Nabokov, he is a joker who prefers not to acknowledge this openly, which is why his

expression is one of passion and discovery. He does, however, dare to reveal a pair of hideous or perhaps damaged knees and to wear a cap inadmissible in someone who never actually became a real American. He is in his Bermuda shorts, pretending to be hunting a butterfly, but his shirt pocket is full of pens or glasses or something: some object inappropriate for a person out hunting. He is already an old man, but this is evident not so much from his excited face as from the fact that he is wearing a cardigan. Besides, no one ever bagged anything while standing with one hand on his hips.

If Djuna Barnes is the most distinguished and T.E. Lawrence the most plebeian, then Thomas Hardy is the most rustic-looking member of the collection. James aside (at the other extreme) he is the only one who does not look anything like a writer, not at least in this photo taken in old age, in which the thick, buttoned-up

woollen waistcoat and weather-beaten skin (it looks like wood), the lashless eyelids, overgrown eyebrows, and straw-like moustache transform him into a country doctor whose disgruntled expression could as easily be due to an enforced and unwanted retirement as to having been a witness to far too many gloomy stories, "life's little ironies," as he called them. By this time, Hardy had already abandoned prose for poetry, and yet he looks anything but a poet. When you think that he would live a further fourteen years, it makes you shudder to imagine what state that lined skin would be in by then. Or perhaps, given that he was a rustic, it had always been like that, ever since youth.

Yeats is undeniably a poet, even though, in the photo, his hair is already white and one does not tend to associate old men with the writing of poetry. When you see that face, you see a fanatic or a visionary, someone with too strong a character, convinced about everything he does or thinks; it is a very authentic face. The dishevelled hair saves him from seeming old and looks almost fair or blond, it lends movement and brio to the whole face; he is a man with a superabundance of energy. The dark eyebrows are also striking; and the invisible gaze that can only be guessed at behind the glasses, means that he seems to be looking, in fact, with those firm lips of his, as if he were nothing but voice.

Unlike Yeats, Eliot's face could easily be that of an essayist, not to say—which would be cheating—the face of a bank clerk, since we know that is what he was. He is a man who has spent decades combing his hair in exactly the same way, and he does not care in the least that his slicked-down hair emphasises his jug-handle ears, for he is aware that they are what lend singularity to his head. He is meticulous, a perfectionist, and he does not find it an effort to remain so immaculate—it is just a question of habit. He has

the serene, trusting look of someone who has scarcely any doubts about the world order, because he is basically in agreement with it and will contribute to maintaining it. Nevertheless, his whole face exudes a strange, almost vehement sense of hope, and that is why he could also be an inventor.

Melville is, to be honest, something of a disappointment: he looks like a caricature of himself, that is, of the man whom one would guarantee to have been the author of *Moby Dick*, although less so of *Bartleby* or *Billy Budd*. His torso is in shadow or, rather, shaded off, as if to emphasise still more the one thing that really counts in that face, the very long, patriarchal, overly patriarchal beard. This  venerable gentleman, whose portrait is exactly contemporary with the two of Wilde, is his polar opposite, his condemnation and his negation, with his short, grey, crimped hair, the undisguised space between his eyes where his eyebrows meet and where the hair is less grey, and that misty look in his left eye and the authoritarian look in his right, as diffuse, in short, as the modest jacket of which one can make out only one button, a very high button. Melville is, in this photo, a grandfather, or a Quaker, or a pilgrim, or a national treasure, or, which is worse, a symbolic character out of one of his own books.

Despite the fierce look, Mayakovsky does not look authoritarian, he appears, instead, defenceless. It is like a still from an American movie rather than a Russian one, a major criminal caught in the lens of the law. He is pictured against a wall, as if he were Public Enemy Number One, or, rather, the enemy cornered just before his perfectly legal street execution, with no

trial. He is holding not a weapon, but some sheets of paper, and that is the only thing that seems out of keeping with his otherwise harmonious figure, unless the sheets of paper are not, as one fears and regrets, poems, but pamphlets he was reading to a crowd from a platform. He is an ill-tempered or perhaps a hounded man, but, as revealed by that determinedly wide stance, unwilling to give in or surrender even if they riddle him with bullets. The most striking and most resolute thing of all, however, are his shoes, so remarkable that they slightly invade the turn-ups of his beautifully pressed trousers: one could not give up such shoes even at the moment of death.

They are the main object in the photo of Beckett too, except that their owner, seated almost on the floor and in a corner, seems slightly terrified of them. He is another hounded man, but at least he is not surprised by the hounding: he's ready for it; he is holding a cigarette in his right hand and his left hand seems to be adorned, incongruously for someone so sober, with a bracelet rather than a wristwatch. His clothes are nothing out of the ordinary, although his cufflinks look like handcuffs. If it weren't for those large shoes, the only thing that would matter, as in any portrait of Beckett, would be his head and those eagle eyes, which

stare straight out with a truly animal expression, as if they did not understand the need for this moment of eternity, or why anyone should want to photograph it. Beckett's is a recent death, and that is why, I think, his eyes seem more alive than those of the others.

Thomas Bernhard's death is almost as recent, and there are no postcards of him, although this photo may perhaps look like a postcard and is one of the most moving in the whole collection. Despite his not particularly attractive, slightly coarse features (they became more refined with age), and the over-long sideburns that betray the date when the photo must have been taken, his face, because of his eyes, is one of the kindest, most humorous, intelligent, and sympathetic in the gallery. The left hand stroking his

face seems, at first, to have adopted an excessively artificial pose, but that initial effect is cancelled out when you notice that his little finger, which is about to push itself in between his lips, underlines the authenticity of this peaceful meditation. That gaze is not of wonderment, but of learning, and is so clear that it erases everything else, the broad bald head and the large nose. "So that's how it is," his alert gaze seems to be thinking.

The deadest of all, though, is William Blake, who is not even himself, but his own mask. That mask, however, was made not from his corpse, but from life, as the postcard tells us: *Plaster-cast from a life-mask, 1823,* four years before he actually died. Just as others pretended to be writing or thinking in order to have their portrait taken, Blake is pretending to be dead. Not that he does it very well, for if you look closely at this mask on a pedestal, those closed eyes could not possibly be those of a dead man, because they are squeezed tight shut, as if they could still see, but did not want to. The nostrils are holding their breath. The forehead is taut, as if full of palpitating veins. The lips do not exist, they are just a long, firm line, drawn in one movement, and there is tension in that line. Blake pre-

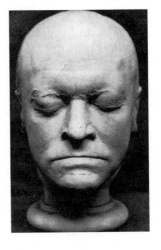

tended to be dead while alive, and now that he really is dead, he can still deceive us: he is a man in control of his posterity. He is a mixture of the living and the dead, which is why his portrait is that of the most perfect of artists.

"Written Lives": William Faulkner, 1958, photo by Ralph Thompson; Joseph Conrad, 1916; Isak Dinesen, photo by Rie Nissen; James Joyce, 1926, photo by Berenice Abbott; Tomasi di Lampedusa and his wife, c. 1930, photo by Giuseppe Biancheri; Henry James, c. 1898; Arthur Conan Doyle, 1928; Robert Louis Stevenson, c. 1892; Ivan Turgenev, 1879; Thomas Mann, photo by Alfred A. Knopf; Vladimir Nabokov, 1929; Rainer Maria Rilke, 1900; Malcolm Lowry, 1932; Mme du Deffand; Rudyard Kipling, 1882, photo by Bourne & Shepherd; Arthur Rimbaud, painting by Jef Robson; Djuna Barnes, 1933, photo by Carl van Vechten; Oscar Wilde, 1897, courtesy of William Andrews Clark Library; Yukio Mishima; Laurence Sterne, aquarelle by Louis Carmontelle. "Fugitive Women": Lady Hester Stanhope, lithograph by Day & Haghe; Vernon Lee, 1889, drawing by John Singer Sargent; Adah Isaacs Menken, 1866, photo by Sarony; Violet Hunt, c. 1910, photo by E.O. Hoppé; Julie de Lespinasse; Emily Brontë, painting by Patrick Branwell Brontë.

"Perfect Artists": *Charles Dickens*: photographer unknown; Dickens reading to his daughters (National Portrait Gallery); photo by Herbert Watkins, 1859 (National Portrait Gallery). *Stéphane Mallarmé*: photo by Nadar; oil painting by Édouard Manet, 1876 (Réunion des musées nationaux). *Oscar Wilde*: both photos by Napoleon Sarony, 1882. *Charles Baudelaire*: photographer unknown; photo by Étienne Carjat, c. 1863. (Arch. Phot. Paris/S.P.A.D.E.M.). *Henry James*: oil painting by John Singer Sargent, 1913 (National Portrait Gallery); Henry and William James, photographer unknown. *Laurence Sterne*: oil painting by Sir Joshua Reynolds, 1760 (National Portrait Gallery); marble bust by J. Nollekens, 1766 (National Portrait Gallery). *André Gide*: photographer unknown; Doc. Roger-Viollet. *Joseph Conrad*: photo by Malcolm Arbuthnot, 1924. *William Faulkner*: photos by Hy Peskin, 1953 and 1962, Time Inc.; photo by Henri Cartier-Bresson, 1947. *Jorge Luis Borges*: photo by Grete Stern, 1951. *Rainer Maria Rilke*: photographer unknown. *Edgar Allen Poe*: photographer unknown. *Friedrich Nietzsche*: the author and his mother, photographer unknown; photographer unknown. *T.E. Lawrence*: photographer unknown (National Portrait Gallery); photographer unknown, 1927 (J.M. Wilson); photographer unknown, c. 1928. (National Portrait Gallery). *Djuna Barnes*: photo by Berenice Abbott, 1985 (Parasol Press). *Mark Twain*: photo by Underwood & Underwood. *Vladimir Nabokov*: photo by Philippe Halsman (Hastings Galleries Collection). *Thomas Hardy*: photogravure by Emil Otto Hoppé, c. 1913-1914 (National Portrait Gallery); *William Butler Yeats*: photo by Howard Coster, 1935 (National Portrait Gallery). *T.S. Eliot*: photo by Emil Otto Hoppé, 1919. *Herman Melville*: photo by Rockwood, c. 1885. *Samuel Beckett*: photo by Jerry Bauer, 1964. *Thomas Bernhard*: photographer unknown. *William Blake*: plaster mask by J.S. Deville, 1823 (National Portrait Gallery).

Bibliography

Acton, Harold: *Memoirs of an Aesthete*, Methuen, London, 1970.
——. *More Memoirs of an Aesthete*, Methuen, London, 1970.
Adlard, John: *Stenbock, Yeats and the Nineties*, Cecil & Amelia Woolf,
    London, 1969.
——. *Christmas with Count Stenbock*, Enitharmon Press, London, 1980.
Amis, Kingsley: *Rudyard Kipling*, Thames & Hudson, London, 1975.
Andreas-Salomé, Lou: *Mirada retrospectiva* (translated by Alejandro
    Venegas), Alianza, Madrid, 1980.
Baretti, Giuseppe: *Scritti*, Einaudi, Turin, 1976.
Barnes, Djuna: *New York*, Sun & Moon Press, Los Angeles, 1989.
——. *I Could Never Be Lonely without a Husband*, Virago, London, 1985.
Bjørnvig, Thornkild: *The Pact, My Friendship with Isak Dinesen*, Souvenir
    Press, London, 1984.
Blixen, Karen: *Out of Africa*, Penguin, Harmondsworth, 1979.
Bowles, Paul: *Without Stopping, An Autobiography*, The Ecco Press, New York,
    1985.
Carpenter, Humphrey: *Geniuses Together*, Unwin, London, 1987.
Carr, John Dickson: *The Life of Sir Arthur Conan Doyle*, Harper, New York,
    1949.
Conrad, Jessie: *Joseph Conrad As I Knew Him*, Garden City, New York, 1926.
Conrad, Joseph: *Conrad's Prefaces*, Dent, London, 1937.
——. *The Mirror of the Sea, Memories and Impressions*, Methuen, London,
    1926.
——. *A Personal Record*, Nelson, London, n.d.
——. *Congo Diary and Other Uncollected Pieces*, Garden City, New York,
    1978.
——. *El espejo del mar* [*The Mirror of the Sea*] (translated by Javier Marías,
    foreword by Juan Benet), Hiperión, Madrid, 1982.
Cowley, Malcolm: *The Faulkner-Cowley File, Letters and Memories, 1944-1962*,
    Penguin, Harmondsworth, 1978.
——. *Writers at Work, First Series*, Penguin, Harmondsworth, 1977.
Craveri, Benedetta: *Madame du Deffand e il suo mondo*, Adelphi, Milan, 1982.
Croft-Cooke, Rupert: *Feasting with Panthers*, Holt Rinehart & Winston,
    New York, 1967.
Cross, Wilbur L.: *The Life and Times of Laurence Sterne*, Russell & Russell,
    New York, 1967.
Curle, Richard: *The Last Twelve Years of Joseph Conrad*, Garden City, New
    York, 1928.
——. *Joseph Conrad, A Study*, Kegan Paul, London 1914.
Daiches, David: *Robert Louis Stevenson and His World*, Thames & Hudson,

London, 1973.

Day, Douglas: *Malcolm Lowry, A Biography*, Oxford University Press, Oxford, 1984.

Deffand, Madame du: *Cher Voltaire*, Des femmes, Paris, 1987.

——. *Lettres à H. Walpole, Voltaire et quelques autres*, Plasma, Paris, 1979.

Dinesen, Isak: *Letters from Africa, 1914-1931*, Picador, London, 1979.

——. *Daguerreotypes and Other Essays*, Heinemann, London, 1979.

——. *On Modern Marriage and Other Observations*, St Martin's Press, New York, 1986.

——. *Ehrengard* (foreword and translation by Javier Marías), Bruguera, Barcelona, 1984.

Douglas, Lord Alfred: *Oscar Wilde, A Summing-Up*, The Richards Press, London, 1950.

Doyle, Arthur Conan Doyle: *Memories and Adventures*, Oxford University Press, Oxford, 1989.

——. *The Great Boer War*, Smith, Elder & Co., London, 1900.

Edel, Leon: *The Life of Henry James* (2 vols.), Penguin, Harmondsworth, 1977.

Ellmann, Richard: *Oscar Wilde*, Hamish Hamilton, London, 1987.

——. *Four Dubliners*, George Braziller, New York, 1987.

Faulkner, John: *My Brother Bill*, Gollancz, London, 1964.

Faulkner, William: *Essays, Speeches and Public Letters*, Chatto & Windus, London, 1967.

——. *Mayday*, University of Notre Dame Press, Notre Dame, 1978.

——. *Selected Letters* (ed. Joseph Blotner), Vintage, New York, 1978.

——. *Helen: A Courtship & Mississippi Poems*, Tulane University & Yoknapatawpha Press, New Orleans & Yoknapatawpha, 1981.

——. *Si yo amaneciera otra vez* [*If I should rouse again*], Javier Marías (with 12 poems by William Faulkner, translated by Javier Marías), Alfaguara, Madrid, 1997.

——. *Últimos cuentos* [*Last Tales*] (translated by Alejandro Vilafranca del Castillo, foreword by Javier Marías), Debate, Madrid, 1990.

Field, Andrew: *Djuna: The Formidable Miss Barnes*, University of Texas Press, Austin, 1985.

Flaubert, Gustave: *Correspondance* (3 vols.), Gallimard, Paris, 1973, 1980, 1991.

Flaubert, Gustave & Tourguéniev, Ivan: *Correspondance*, Flammarion, Paris, 1989.

Fluchère, Henri: *Laurence Sterne, de l'homme à l'oeuvre*, Gallimard, Paris, 1961.

Ford, Madox Ford: *Return to Yesterday*, Liveright, New York, 1972.

——. *Portraits from Life*, Houghton Mifflin, Boston, 1980.

——. *Memories and Impressions*, Penguin, Harmondsworth, 1979.

———. *Joseph Conrad, A Personal Remembrance*, The Ecco Press, New York, 1989.

Gide, André: *Oscar Wilde in memoriam (Souvenirs)*, Mercure de France, Paris, 1989.

———. *Journal 1889-1939*, Gallimard, Paris, 1986.

———. *Journal 1939-1949 & Souvenirs*, Gallimard, Paris, 1984.

Gilmour, David: *The Last Leopard*, Collins Harvill, London, 1998.

Hall-Stevenson, John: *Yorick's Sentimental Journey Continued*, The Georgian Society, London, 1902.

Hardy, Thomas: *El brazo marchito* [*The Withered Arm*] (translated by Javier Marías), Alianza, Madrid, 1984.

Harris, Frank: *Contemporary Portraits, First Series*, Mitchell Kennerley, New York, 1915.

———. *Contemporary Portraits, Second Series*, Published by the author, New York, 1919.

———. *Contemporary Portraits, Third Series*, Published by the author, New York, n.d.

———. *Contemporary Portraits, Fourth Series*, Grant Richards, London, 1924.

Hyde, H. Montgomery: *Henry James at Home*, Methuen, London, 1969.

———. "The Lamb House Library of Henry James" in *The Book Collector*, Volume 16, No. 4, Winter 1967.

James, Alice: *Diary*, Penguin, Harmondsworth, 1982.

James, Henry: *The Complete Notebooks*, Oxford University Press, Oxford, 1987.

———. *Autobiography*, Princeton University Press, Princeton, 1983.

———. *Within the Rim*, Collins, London, 1918.

———. *A Little Tour of France*, Oxford University Press, Oxford, 1984.

———. *English Hours*, Oxford University Press, Oxford, 1981.

———. *Italian Hours*, Grove Press, New York, 1979.

———. *Parisian Sketches*, Rupert Hart-Davis, London, 1948.

James, Henry & Stevenson, Robert Louis: *A Record of Friendship and Criticism*, Rupert Hart-Davis, London, 1948.

James, Henry & Wells, H.G.: *A Record of their Friendship, their Debate on the Art of Fiction, and their Quarrel*, Rupert Hart-Davis, London, 1958.

Joyce, Stanislaus: *My Brother's Keeper*, Faber & Faber, London, 1982.

Joyce, James: *Scritti italiani*, Mondadori, Milan, 1979.

———. *Selected Letters* (ed. Richard Ellmann), The Viking Press, New York,

———. *Critical Writings*, Faber & Faber, London, 1959.

Kipling, Rudyard: *Something of Myself*, Penguin, Harmondsworth, 1977.

———. *Stalky & Co.*, Macmillan, London, 1982.

Lampedusa, Tomasso Giuseppe di: *Lezioni su Stendhal*, Sellerio, Palermo, 1987.

————. *Letteratura inglese, Volume primo*, Mondadori, Milan, 1990.

————. *Letteratura inglese, Volume secondo*, Mondadori, Milan, 1991.

Laver, James: *Oscar Wilde*, The British Council, London, 1954.

Lee, Vernon: *The Handling of Words*, The Bodley Head, London, 1923.

Legallienne, Richard: *The Romantic '90s*, Putnam, London, 1951.

Ligne, Prince de: *Mémoires, lettres et pensées*, François Bourin, Paris, 1989.

Lottman, Herbert: *Gustave Flaubert* (translated by Marianne Véron), Fayard, Paris, 1989.

Lowry, Malcolm: *Selected Letters*, Penguin, Harmondsworth, 1985.

Mann, Thomas: *Diarios, 1918-1936* (edited and translated by Pedro Gálvez), Plaza & Janés, Barcelona, 1986.

————. *Diarios, 1937-1939* (edited and translated by Pedro Gálvez), Plaza & Janés.

————. *Letters* (selected and translated by Richard and Clara Winston), Penguin, Harmondsworth, 1975.

————. *Los orígenes del Doctor Faustus (La novela de una novela)* (translated by Pedro Gálvez), Alianza, Madrid, 1976.

————. *Travesía marítima con Don Quijote* (translated by Antonio de Zubiaurre), Júcar, Madrid, 1974.

Mann, Thomas: *Relato de mi vida*, & Mann, Erika: *El último año de mi padre* (translated by Andrés Sánchez Pascual), Alianza, Madrid, 1969.

Meriwether, James & Milgate, Michael (eds.): *Lion in the Garden, Interviews with William Faulkner, 1926-1962*, University of Nebraska Press, Lincoln, 1980.

Mishima, Yukio: *Confessions of a Mask* (translated by Meredith Weatherby), Panther, Frogmore, 1977.

————. *On Hagakure: The Samurai Ethic and Modern Japan* (translated by Kathryn Sparling), Penguin, Harmondsworth, 1979.

Nabokov, Vladimir: *Speak, Memory, An Autobiography Revisited*, Penguin, Harmondsworth, 1982.

————. *Strong Opinions*, McGraw-Hill, New York, 1981.

————. *Lectures on Russian Literature*, Picador, London, 1983.

————. *Lectures on Literature*, Harcourt Brace Jovanovich, New York, 1983.

————. *Desde que te vi morir*, Javier Marías (with 18 poems by Vladimir Nabokov translated by Javier Marías), Alfaguara, Madrid, 1999.

Orlando, Francesco: *Ricordo di Lampedusa*, Vanni Scheiwiller, Milan, 1985

Osbourne, Katherine Durham: *Robert Louis Stevenson in California*, A.C. McClurg, Chicago, 1911.

Plimpton, George (ed): *Writers at Work, Fourth Series*, Penguin, Harmondsworth, 1982.

Pound, Ezra: *Pound/Joyce*, New Directions, New York, 1987.

Praz, Mario: *Studi e svaghi inglesi* (2 vols.), Garzanti, Milan, 1983.

————. *Il patto col serpente*, Mondadori, Milan, 1973.

Prokosch, Frederic: *Voices*, Farrar Straus Giroux, New York, 1983.

Rilke, Rainer Maria: *Correspondance* (translated by Blaise Briod, Philippe Jaccottet and Pierre Klossowski), Seuil, Paris, 1976.

———. *Journaux de jeunesse* (translated by Philippe Jaccottet), Seuil, Paris, 1989.

———. *Lettres sur Cézanne* (translated by Philippe Jaccottet), Seuil, Paris, 1991.

———. *Lettres françaises à Merline, 1919-1922*, Seuil, Paris, 1984.

———. *Lettres à une amie vénitienne*, Gallimard, Paris, 1985.

———. *El testamento* (translated by Feliu Formosa), Alianza, Madrid, 1976.

———. *Epistolario español* (translated by Jaime Ferreiro Alemparte), Espasa Calpe, Madrid, 1976.

———. *Antología poética* (translated by Jaime Ferreiro Alemparte), Espasa Calpe, Madrid, 1968.

Rimbaud, Arthur: *Oeuvres complètes*, Gallimard, Paris, 1963.

———. *Je suis ici dans les Gallas*, Éditions du Rocher, Monaco, 1991.

———. *Lettres de la vie littéraire*, Gallimard, Paris, 1990.

Russell, Bertrand: *Portraits from Memory and Other Essays*, George Allen & Unwin, London, 1956.

Smith, Timothy d'Arch: *Love in Earnest*, Routledge & Kegan Paul, London, 1970.

Starkie, Enid: *Arthur Rimbaud* (translated by José Luis López Muñoz), Siruela, Madrid, 1989.

Sterne, Laurence: *The Life and Opinions of Tristram Shandy, Gentleman*, J.L. Legrand, Basle, 1792.

———. *A Sentimental Journey through France and Italy*, J.G.A. Stoupe, Paris, 1780.

———. *A Sentimental Journey & The Journal to Eliza*, Dent, London, 1969.

———. *Second Journal to Eliza*, G. Bell, London, 1929.

———. *Letters* (ed. Lewis Perry Curtis), Oxford University Press, Oxford, 1965.

———. *La vida y las opiniones del caballero Tristram Shandy & Los sermones de Mr Yorick* [*The Life and Opinions of Tristram Shandy, Gentleman & The Sermons of Mr. Yorick*] (translated by Javier Marías, foreword by Andrew Wright), Alfaguara, Madrid, 1999.

Stevenson, Robert Louis: *Ethical Studies & Edinburgh: Picturesque Notes*, Heinemann, London, 1924.

———. *Memories and Portraits & Memoirs of Himself & Selections from His Notebook*, Heinemann, London, 1924.

———. *Further Memories*, Heinemann, London, 1924.

———. *Memoir of Fleeming Jenkin & Records of a Family of Engineers*, Heinemann, London, 1924.

———. *Letters* (5 vols.), Heinemann, London, 1924.

——. *An Inland Voyage & Travels with a Donkey in the Cevennes*, Heinemann, London, 1924.

——. *The Amateur Emigrant & The Silverado Squatters*, Heinemann, London, 1924.

——. *De vuelta del mar* [*Home from the Sea*] (translated by Javier Marías), Hiperión, Madrid, 1980.

Stokes, Henry Scott: *The Life and Death of Yukio Mishima*, Farrar Straus Giroux, New York, 1982.

Strachey, Giles Lytton: *Biographical Essays*, Harcourt Brace & World, New York, n.d.

Svendsen, Clara (ed.): *Isak Dinesen, A Memorial*, Random House, New York, 1965.

Tour et Taxis, Princesse de la: *Souvenirs sur Rainer Maria Rilke*, Obsidiane, Belleville-sur-Vie, 1987.

Traugott, John: *Tristram Shandy's World*, Russell & Russell, New York, 1970.

Turgenev, Ivan: *Sketches from a Hunter's Album* (selected and translated by Richard Freeborn), Penguin, Harmondsworth, 1977.

——. *Rudin* (translated by Richard Freeborn), Penguin, Harmondsworth, 1979.

——. *Literary Reminiscences and Autobiographical Fragments* (translated by David Magarshack, with an essay by Edmund Wilson), Faber & Faber, London, 1984

Van Vechten, Carl: *Letters* (ed. Bruce Kellner), Yale University Press, New Haven, 1987.

Walpole, Horace: *Selected Letters*, Dent, London, 1967.

——. *Days of the Dandies*, The Grolier Society, London, n.d.

Wharton, Edith: *A Backward Glance*, Century, London, 1987.

Wilde, Oscar: *Letters* (ed. Rupert Hart-Davis), Rupert Hart-Davis, London, 1963.

——. *More Letters* (ed. Rupert Hart-Davis), The Vanguard Press, New York, 1985.

Yeats, William Butler: *El crepúsculo celta* [*The Celtic Twilight*] (translated by Javier Marías), Alfaguara, Madrid, 1985.

Yourcenar, Marguerite: *Mishima ou la vision du vide*, Gallimard, Paris, 1989.